Kevin Basconi is a man full of the Spirit are open to perceive the realms of heav LORD JESUS! In the Book of Ephesians, been given every spiritual blessing in the heavenlies through Jesus the Christ. In the original language the heavenlies can be interpreted territories, domains, and realms. As you read this book by Kevin, the SPIRIT of revelation will be released to you and you will entertain heaven through prayer praise and worship. You will know the will of God and the FATHER as well as JESUS more deeply and intimately for your life!

PASTOR TONY KEMP
Tony Kemp Ministries

"There is a rapid acceleration in heaven preparing God's people for the last, great move of God. This is why the veil between heaven and earth is getting thinner and that is why so many people today are accessing heaven. Accessing heaven is available to you today. God wants all your prayers answered by receiving heavenly revelation.

SID ROTH
Host, *It's Supernatural!*"

I have several friends who repeatedly tell me, "If you can see it, you can have it." There is much truth to that statement; and in his new book, *Entertaining Heaven to Become Triumphant in Prayer*, Kevin Basconi teaches and shows us how to see into the realm of eternity, or the heavenly realms. Often times, we reduce the scriptures to meet our present experience. Kevin challenges us to bring our experience up to what the Bible says! There are so many scriptures inviting us to see what is taking place in heaven. As we see into that realm, faith is released in us to believe God for the unbelievable, to trust Him for the unattainable. God really will and does answer our prayers! Do you want to be "triumphant in prayer"? Of course you do, and so do I! Apply the principles that Kevin highlights in this book and learn to see released on the earth what you see in heaven.

ALAN KOCH
Senior and Founding Pastor of Christ Triumphant Church

Wow! is all I can say for this new book by Kevin Basconi entitled *Entertaining Heaven to Become Triumphant in Prayer*. The spiritual truths and revelation in this book act as a school of the supernatural and are easy to understand. You will receive impartation from the Holy Spirit as you read, and you can expect your personal time with the Lord to accelerate in new realms of glory. This book is sure to be a staple for every hungry believer.

JEFF JANSEN
Founder of Global Fire Ministries International

Once again, Kevin Basconi has written a brilliant gem of a book, this time concerning effective prayers from the perspective of God's throne in heaven. This book has the potential to change your approach to God on a daily basis and lead you by revelation into a glorious experience of His manifest presence and supernatural provision. Get it. Read it. Do it!

JOAN HUNTER
Author/Healing Evangelist

Kevin Basconi is one of the most outstanding revelatory teachers on the Kingdom realms that I know. He has a passion to see every believer walk in the fullness of the glory, and it comes through in his teachings. In his latest book, *Entertaining Heaven to Become Triumphant in Prayer*, you will discover profound keys to engaging the manifest presence of Jesus to see answers to your prayer life. I highly recommend this book as it will transport you to a higher dimension and shift you to a place of manifestations in God.

PROPHET CHARLIE SHAMP
Destiny Encounters International www.destinyencounters.com

Kevin is someone who I trust listens to the voice of the Lord constantly. His value for discernment has made a big impact on my life. Through obedience and right discernment, the Lord has given him much revelation on the Kingdom of Heaven. His many encounters with Jesus and the kingdom of God have allowed him to see what the Father is doing on the earth and to think as our Lord Jesus Christ thinks. This book brings you to the reality of heaven and the access we have through Jesus Christ, so that we too can taste and see the Lord is good and we may know how to bring heaven to touch the earth as Jesus did.

ROBERT WARD
Redding, CA

Kevin Basconi has done it again! His new book, *Entertaining Heaven to Become Triumphant in Prayer*, shares revelation and keys to experiencing and walking in the heavenly realms. This fast paced book gives you practical and real guidance in how to release and discern the reality and power of answered prayer. We are living in a day of great spiritual activity and, as Kevin shares, in this book, there is an open invitation for you to entertain heaven now! Every reader will find themselves stirred and empowered to experience the heavenly nature of God for themselves.

CAROL KOCH
Founder and Director of Children on the Frontlines

ENTERTAINING HEAVEN
TO BECOME TRIUMPHANT IN PRAYER

KEVIN & KATHY BASCONI

Entertaining HEAVEN To Become Triumphant In Prayer
by Kevin Basconi

ISBN: 978-0-9989122-2-6

King of Glory Ministries International Publications 2017
King of Glory Ministries International
PO Box 903, Moravian Falls, NC 28654, 336-818-1210

www.kingofgloryministries.org

No part of this book may be reproduced or transmitted in any form or by any means—electronic or mechanical, including photocopying, recording, or by any information storage and retrieval system—without written permission from the authors except as provided by the copyright laws of the United States of America. Unauthorized reproduction is a violation of federal as well as spiritual laws.

Unless otherwise noted, all Scripture quotations are from the New King James Version of the Bible. Copyright © 1979, 1980, 1982 by Thomas Nelson, Inc., publishers. Used by permission.

Scripture quotations marked AMP are from the Amplified Bible. Copyright © 1954, 1958, 1962, 1964, 1965, 1987 by The Lockman Foundation. Used by permission.

Scripture quotations marked KJV are from the King James Version of the Bible.

Greek definitions are derived from Strong's Greek Concordance.

Hebrew definitions are derived from Strong's Hebrew Concordance.

Copyright 2017 by Kevin Basconi

All rights reserved.

This Book is dedicated to God the Father, God the Son, and God the Holy Spirit. Without You Guys none of this would have been possible!

Table of Contents

Acknowledgements xi

PART ONE
You and Entertaining the Heavenly Places

INTRODUCTION 1
Heaven and You 3

CHAPTER 1
Understanding Heavenly Realms 9

CHAPTER 2
Heavenly Prayer: Discerning Heaven's Heart 15

CHAPTER 3
Heaven Is Real 21

CHAPTER 4
Heavenly Dimensions 33

CHAPTER 5
Heavenly Perspectives 43

CHAPTER 6
Discerning Heavenly Places 49

CHAPTER 7
Heavenly Revelation and Earthly Manifestation 59

CHAPTER 8
God's Angels and the Invisible Realms of the Heavenly Places 69

CHAPTER 9
God Created the Invisible Realms of Heaven 77

CHAPTER 10
The Hidden and Mysterious Treasures of the Kingdom of Heaven 87

Part Two
Visions of the Heavenly Places

Introduction 2
Visions of Heaven 103

Chapter 11
The Father's House 107

Chapter 12
The Great Banquet Hall 115

Chapter 13
The Feast 119

Chapter 14
Entertaining Heaven 123

Chapter 15
Millions of Angels 131

Chapter 16
A Heavenly Place: The Vault of Spare Body Parts 135

Chapter 17
Working with Angels of Healings and Creative Miracles 141

Chapter 18
The River of Revelation 145

Chapter 19
The Sword of the Lord 151

Chapter 20
Jesus Loves the Little Children 153

Chapter 21
The Greatest in the Kingdom of Heaven 159

Chapter 22
The Lord's Manicured Gardens 167

Chapter 23
The Lion of Judah 177

Chapter 24
The Pathways of the Lord 179

CHAPTER 25
The Water of Life 183

CHAPTER 26
The Fountain of Living Waters..191

CHAPTER 27
The Father's Vineyard...195

CHAPTER 28
Heavenly Parables and an Answered Prayer 203

CHAPTER 29
The Throne Room..211

CHAPTER 30
The Lord's Righteous Judgments and Eternal Grace....................217

CHAPTER 31
The Author and Finisher of Faith...223

CHAPTER 32
God's Unconditional, Unimaginable, and Indescribable Love....227

Prayer Index..233
Notes...239
Contact the Authors...241
About the Authors and King of Glory Ministries International...........243
Other Books by Kevin Basconi 246

Acknowledgements

I want to thank my wonderful precious wife, Kathy Basconi. Thank you for your enduring and everlasting love, your Christ-like kindness, your amazing patience, and for the long hours of proofreading. Thank you for your help and support with the entire process of writing this book.

You are more precious than rubies, and nothing that I may desire can compare with you or your love.

I love you!

Thank you for walking through the valleys and upon the mountain tops with me!

Every day that I invest with you on this side of eternity is like heaven to me.

Other than Jesus Christ, you are the most wonderful thing that God has placed in my life.

Part One

You and Entertaining the Heavenly Places

INTRODUCTION 1

Heaven and You

Heaven

Is it real?

Is heaven actually a tangible place that we can visit or perhaps even spend eternity?

The truth is that there is a benevolent, kind, and all-loving God who created each of us in His image. As such, the Lord has gone before us to prepare a place or abode for you and me—an eternal place where we will live in God's presence and peace throughout all of eternity. Our spirits will certainly live on forever. God has created us in His very image. As such, we are eternal beings who will inhabit an eternal place called heaven.

God has such an intense and intimate love for you that He sent His only begotten Son that we might have a way to be reunited with Him infinitely (for eternity) in heaven. I am a witness of this. In fact, heaven *is* real. You have been given a wonderful choice and privilege to choose heaven as your eternal home. The descriptions of the heavenly realms and the teachings that I will share in this short book are only mere glimpses into paradise (heaven) or the abode of God. We will spend our days in heaven learning more about God and His Kingdom.

We will continue to grow and mature into the very image and stature of Jesus. For many people this will be the very desire of their hearts. We will grow, learn, and discover much more about the Lord during our time and eternity in heavenly places. We will invest our days exploring and discovering the hidden mysteries of Christ's Kingdom. We will have the privilege to explore the vastness of all of the realms of heaven. We will be given the grace to explore the innumerable heavenly places—places so vast and magnificent that we cannot imagine them with our human minds! I expect that for each of us heaven will be experienced differently. Some may invest eternity fishing in the river of life that flows through Psalm 23. Some may relish investing their time reading in the Father's massive library. Others may seek only to worship the Lord in spirit and in truth around the very throne of God (I share an amazing vision of the throne room later on). And others will pursue the very desires of their heart perfecting their giftings by creating music, literature, and masterpieces of art work in the heavenly places.

On one occasion I saw a very famous artist working on a massive fresco on the ceiling of the banquet hall in heaven. I had the understanding that working like this in the heavenly places was the desire of the person's heart while he had lived upon the earth. This artist even invited me to join him on the scaffold on which he was lying as he completed a detail of a portrait in a fresco. I was overwhelmed at this invitation. And over the course of several months, I watched as the magnificent ceiling fresco was completed in the heavenly places. One day you too will be assigned an activity or supernatural mission in the heavenly places. That is something to think about! You will love what you do there, and every day will be a pleasure that will bring you happiness for eternity!

Yes, heaven is real.

Prepare your heart to learn more about the mysteries of the heavenly places God has prepared for you as we explore heaven together in this testimonial book.

This book is a combination of hermeneutical teachings about heaven and several amazing personal testimonies depicting heavenly encounters or visions of the heavenly places. These depictions of heaven and the heavenly places could rightly be described as ecstatic visions of heaven. During these visionary experiences I entered into a trance or visionary state and time as I understood was suspended. I would enter into these heavenly visions for what seemed to be hours or even whole days at time. These visions continued for an extended season of time. However, when I would "return" to my prayer room, at times only a few hours had passed in the natural realm, though it seemed that I had been in the heavenly places for an entire day or longer.

Allow me to say that since the majority of these experiences unfolded nearly two decades ago I have come to believe that I was translated to heaven in my spirit. The effects of these encounters with the Lord in the heavenly places began to immediately change the difficult circumstances in my life. The Lord took me from poverty to prosperity, from sickness to health, and from hopelessness to hope. As I learned to "entertain heaven," I discovered that the heavenly nature of God was being released into my life and changing my circumstances. In some ways these supernatural transformations were nearly instantaneous. In other cases the impact of these heavenly visions unfolded over the course of time. Some of these manifestations took years and even decades to manifest upon the earth in my life. However, I can say with absolute certainty that all of these supernatural ecstatic visions of heaven and walking with the Lord in the heavenly places drew me closer to the Lord Jesus Christ in relationship as well as understanding of His will for my life.

Allow me to say that that there have been times that Jesus has appeared to me upon the earth. He is not dead. He is alive, and I write this book today as a witness to this fact. I will share that testimony with the reader as well.

What I was saying is that I now believe that I was translated in the spirit, not transported bodily into the realms of heaven. In that place I saw amazing heavenly places. I share several of those heavenly visions with you in the pages of this book. In addition to this I will also share several brief hermeneutical teachings about entertaining heaven today. There is an acceleration of the Lord's plans and agenda for you and for the entire planet Earth unfolding at this moment of time. One aspect of this acceleration of God's plans upon the earth takes the form of a Revelation 4:1 dynamic which John the Revelator penned:

> *After these things I looked, and behold, a door standing open in heaven. And the first voice which I heard was like a trumpet speaking with me, saying, "Come up here, and I will show you things which must take place after this."*

You are living in the day and hour in which the Revelation 4:1 dynamic is accelerating in the lives of people upon the earth.

And the Lord is actually inviting you to "come up here." The Lord is opening the windows and the doors of heaven an inviting His friends to see and discern what must take place after this. In other words, you have an open invitation at this time to "entertain heaven." You have an open invitation to receive divine or heavenly revelation for your life. My prayer is that this book will help you to understand from a biblical perspective how and why discerning and accessing heaven is possible for you today.

My prayer for the reader is that you would learn to "entertain heaven" and perhaps the God of heaven will draw you closer to His Son, Jesus Christ of Nazareth!

Come! Let's begin our exploration of the heavenly places!

CHAPTER 1

Understanding Heavenly Realms

I want to share a few passages of scripture from the Book of John and lay a foundation to help you understand more about heaven and the heavenly realms, or heavenly places. Let's start in John, chapter 1, beginning with verses 1 and 2:

> *In the beginning was the Word, and the Word was with God, and the Word was God. He was in the beginning with God.*

John is speaking about the Lord Jesus Christ. Continuing in verse 3 we read:

> *All things were made through Him, and without Him nothing was made that was made.*

One of the things that will help you to understand heaven in a greater measure is to understand the heavenly dimensions. In 1 John 3, verses 1 and 2 we read:

> *Behold what manner of love the Father has bestowed on us, that we should be called children of God! Therefore the world does not know us, because it did not know Him. Beloved, now we are children of God; and it has not yet been revealed* [made plain or visible] *what we shall be,*

but we know that when He is revealed, we shall be like Him, for we shall see Him as He is.

The word translated "see" in the last sentence is a very special word that means to see with wide open eyes, to perceive, to discern, or to experience. This is what a seer does. It means to see or behold something remarkable, to see something supernatural, or to see with greater than regular sight. Really what John the Revelator is talking about here is what we know as supernatural vision. This is the manifestation of the seer operation in the life of a believer. The seer anointing is not always visual; it may also take the form of spiritual discernment. And we desperately need more discernment in the Body of Christ today to help us ascertain and determine the difference between New Age and real heavenly spiritual encounters. All supernatural encounters must line up with the canon of Scripture as the word of God is the absolute plumb line for our interaction with heaven. Don't be deceived! We will look at this in more detail later in this book. The point being, you can discern heavenly truth correctly without mixture. That is important. This should also be your heart's desire in righteousness and truth (Ephesians 5:9).

If we are going to be able to entertain the heavenly realms on this side of eternity, we need to be able to see and to discern heavenly attributes and heavenly truth. By the grace of God and through the power of the Holy Spirit and the glory of God, many of us have seen the Kingdom of Heaven manifest already. But we see that with our natural vision. These passages of Scripture are referring to a different type of vision. But at times when the Kingdom of Heaven manifests, we can see the results of the heavenly realms invading our space (Earth) though supernatural manifestations like miracles, signs, and wonders. These three should be normal for you as a Spirit-led Christian. Even the ministry of Jesus was confirmed in this manner. We see this in Peter's sermon in Acts 2:21-24 (emphasis added):

> *"...And it shall come to pass That whoever calls on the name of the LORD Shall be saved." Men of Israel, hear these words:* ***Jesus of Nazareth, a Man attested by God to you by miracles, wonders, and signs which God did through Him*** *in your midst, as you yourselves also know—Him, being delivered by the determined purpose and foreknowledge of God, you have taken by lawless hands, have crucified, and put to death; whom God raised up, having loosed the pains of death, because it was not possible that He should be held by it.*

That is some heady stuff! God attested or confirmed the Lord's ministry with accompanying signs. Yes, you are also called to a lifestyle of signs and wonders. Many times this kind of supernatural lifestyle comes upon your life and ministry as you learn to discern, access, or entertain the heavenly realms. Then you just do what you see or discern in heaven like the Lord Jesus (John 5:19; John 3:12-16). You will learn to "see" what the Father is saying to you.

Enlightened

Let's go to Ephesians, chapter 1, verse 18: "*...the eyes of your understanding being enlightened; that you may know what is* *the hope of His calling, what are the riches of the glory of His inheritance in the saints."* The language here is similar to what we saw in the scripture in that the word of God (1 John 1; 1 John 3:1-3) speaks of seeing in a supernatural way. Really it speaks of seeing or discerning a different realm. It speaks of heavenly vision, heavenly knowledge, or supernatural revelation. It speaks of spiritual discernment. The Scripture encourages you and me to discern heaven, though it may not always be visual discernment. (More on this later.)

Scripture is very clear that you can learn to discern heaven or heavenly truth on this side of eternity. In fact, Jesus encouraged you to pray for this manifestation of His Kingdom in the Lord's Prayer, recorded in both Luke 11:2-4 and Matthew 6:9-13. *"In this manner, therefore, pray: Our Father in heaven, Hallowed be Your name. Your kingdom come. Your will be done On earth as it is in heaven"* (Matthew 6:9-10).

Jesus referred to heavenly revelation as our daily bread in Matthew 6:11. I don't know about you, but I do not want to live on stale bread! Stale manna (yesterday's manna) was reported to stink (Exodus 16:20). We need the living word, we need the now or rhema word. We need a fresh word from heaven every day so that our daily bread will become fresh revelation. We need fresh manna just like the manna that God sent to the children of Israel in the desert. Fresh manna (fresh revelation) still comes down from heaven today too! You get your fresh daily bread directly from the heavenly places. I call this kind of supernatural nutrition heavenly revelation, and it is available for you each and every new day if you will only seek the Lord's face for it! You can discern heavenly truth without going to heaven. That is what this book is designed to help you to achieve! Get fresh manna every day!

So, entertaining the heavens is not just about ecstatic visions and encounters with heaven (though these are wonderful). Entertaining heaven is about discerning spiritual truth (revelation or fresh manna) from the God of heaven in your daily life. Entertaining heaven is just about walking as mature sons (or daughters) of God. In the next chapter let's look at how entertaining heaven can transform your life by transforming your prayer life. Learn how to receive immediate answers to your prayers, and learn to pray effectively every day of your life!

CHAPTER 2

Heavenly Prayer: Discerning Heaven's Heart

The disciples discerned and understood that there was a very special grace upon the prayer life of the Lord Jesus Christ. The Lord would go up on to the mountain and pray all night; and when He would come down the next day amazing miracles, creative miracles, signs, and wonders would follow Jesus. We see this in the scripture in Luke 11:1: *"Now it came to pass, as He was praying in a certain place, when He ceased, that one of His disciples said to Him, 'Lord, teach us to pray, as John also taught his disciples.'"*

My prayer for you is that this book will help you to access this kind of heavenly prayer. I pray that as you put the scriptural principles found in these pages to work in your life, your prayers would become not only effectual but powerful and prodigious. May you learn to grab hold of the horns of the altar and develop a lifestyle of answered prayer! How? By learning to allow the precious Holy Spirit to guide and lead you as you pray to the Father in the name of Jesus Christ of Nazareth. As you learn to discern heavenly truth, you will begin to emulate Jesus in your prayer time and pray and minister without doubt or wavering. You will learn to trust in God fully. You will learn that you can actually come boldly before the Father's throne of mercy and grace in the heavenly places (Hebrews 4:16). Answered and effective prayer is one fruit of learning to discern the heavenly realms in your life during your prayer times.

Your Kingdom Come: Supernatural Syncopation

Jesus instructed us to pray like this: *"Your kingdom come. Your will be done On earth as it is in heaven"* (Matthew 6:10). This is not some farfetched theology; this is Bible. It is a real aspect of heaven. This is New Testament Christianity! This is the revealed truth of God to His people through the words of His Son. You can access heaven daily to discern the Lord's will for your life. God can give you His thoughts and revelation (fresh manna) for your life each day in many differing ways. I hope to entertain many of these supernatural methods in the subsequent pages of the book. Heaven can manifest or appear on earth (in our lives) as we pray and align ourselves with heaven. I call this supernatural syncopation. If you can grasp this dynamic of the Lord's Prayer for yourself, it can be life changing! You can learn to become supernaturally syncopated with heaven every day of your life. I ask the Lord what He wants for me to do almost every single day. Guess what? He tells me. And He will tell you too! That is called being led by the Spirit and is an earmark of a mature son (or daughter) of God. You will unquestionably hear the voice of the Lord as He speaks to you. You can discern or receive fresh manna every day as you learn to become supernaturally syncopates with heaven.

If we are going to entertain the heavenly realms, we need to sharpen our spiritual discernment. Everything that we experience and anything that I write in this book must line up with the word of God and the canon of Scripture: **period**. Let me show that to you in the Scripture. Let's look at 1 Corinthians, chapter 2. We are talking about entertaining heaven. The key is not only to entertain heaven but also to access heaven and then to manifest or to release heaven into your sphere of influence. That is answered prayer. That is co-laboring with heaven. Many of us have already seen this Kingdom principle demonstrated where heavenly things are happening in our midst. Where there is an open heaven there is a free flow or access between heaven and earth. This free flow is evident in some individual's lives or at certain gatherings or even certain places. Remember, Jesus was praying in a certain place in Luke 11. The heavenly realms impact or touch the terrestrial realms as heaven touches earth (this is why all of the events that we sponsor are Heaven Touching Earth Gatherings). Look at 1 Corinthians, chapter 2, verse 9, to show you two keys to help you entertain heaven. This is the teaching of the Apostle Paul.

> *But as it is written: "Eye has not seen, nor ear heard, Nor have entered into the heart of man The things which God has prepared for those who love Him."*

What the Apostle Paul is teaching about is the same type of supernatural vision that we have been looking at in 1 John and Ephesians. There is a supernatural vision that God can release to us where our eye can see and our ear can hear in a supernatural or heavenly way. This transpires when we are entertaining heaven. We begin to think from a different perspective. Hallelujah! This is discerning heaven right here, right now, in the now, in the today. Don't be looking and expecting God to do something tomorrow. The Lord is moving today (Hebrews 13:8). Quit making prophetic and pathetic excuses for God not moving in your life and ministries! He is just seeking people who will discern the movement of heaven in their lives and flow with Him. The revival is NOW! Quit wasting time prophesying and looking for a move of God coming tomorrow. He is moving NOW people! Step into it! NOW!

Make a Demand on Heaven

I no longer think the way I used to think. I believe that my God and my Father has engrafted me into His heavenly family and loves me simply because that is who He is and because the Scripture verifies He does. And because He loves me, I believe I can stand up at anytime and anywhere and believe for God to release miracles and healings and signs and wonders at my word. The amazing thing about this type of heavenly mindset is that God backs it up with attesting signs and answered prayers. But, I take a step of faith. I step out and make a demand on heaven. So that is a key for you as well. A key to heavenly realms is to make a demand on heaven in the now.

New Homes

In 2004 the Lord (the Holy Spirit) told me to begin to pray for "new homes." I thought, "Gee, I just need one home, Lord," and began to pray that way. But the Lord quickly and gently impressed upon me that He had instructed me to pray for new home(s) plural. So I was obedient. Though it did not make any sense to me, I began to pray for home(s) plural. I was praying amiss when I was only praying for one new home. That is one reason most of our prayers are not answered (James 4:3). Even though I did not understand the Lord's directives, I began to call those things that were not as if they were (Romans 4:17). In my prayer room I have a dry erase board and I have home(s) written on it.

Today, in 2018, there are four check marks beside the word *home(s)* on that board in my prayer room. Why? Because the Lord has led and allowed me to own four different homes in the last fourteen years. This does not count or include the other seven homes that we have built for orphaned children in East Africa! *"Not my will be done, but Your will be done, on earth as it is in heaven."* Is not God amazing! Seventeen years ago I could not even afford a toothbrush while on a mission's trip! I hope that this illustration is helpful to you and encourages your faith. For if I boast in anything, I boast in Christ Jesus! I boast in the Holy Spirit who can lead us in prayer. I boast in my Heavenly Father who answers our prayers when we are supernaturally syncopated with heaven, or entertaining heaven.

So again, 1 Corinthians, chapter 2, verse 9, speaks of our eyes and our ears. That is a key to entertaining heavenly realms. In other words, we need to begin to see and hear in a new and supernatural way, as we saw outlined in 1 John and Ephesians. Again this is the operation of the seer function, which is also spiritual discernment. (Forgive me for being repetitive, but I have learned that we can receive spiritual truth by having it come into our eye gates repeatedly.) Repetition births revelation and revelation births the reality of His power and the Kingdom of God in your life. So there you go! I believe many of you are reading this book because God wants to change the way you think, He wants to change the way you see, and He wants to change the way you hear. Right now, just purpose in your heart and spirit to *"believe to receive"* as you read this book!

Spiritually Discerned

In 1 Corinthians, chapter 2, verse 14, we read: *"But the natural man does not receive the things of the Spirit of God, for they are foolishness to him...."* Our carnal mind has a difficult time comprehending the attributes of heaven and the supernatural operations of our heavenly Father. Why? Because all of our lives, ever since the time we've been little tots, we've been taught that the things of the Spirit are foolishness. But our Father wants to change our minds so that we understand that the heavenly things are more real than the terrestrial things.

The Lord is actively searching for someone who will allow the Holy Spirit to transform their minds. The Lord is actively looking for people who He can teach how to align themselves correctly with heaven. God is seeking people who are supernaturally syncopated with heaven through simple faith. How does that happen? We see it in the second half of verse 14: *"... nor can he know them, because they are spiritually discerned."* We are talking about developing our spiritual discernment to entertain or interact with heaven. And God the Father, God the Son, and God the Holy Spirit will help you to become truly Spirit led and to entertain or interact with heaven. In fact, that is the whole reason for your existence! In the next chapter I will share several more supernatural keys that can unlock heaven and revival in your life now!

CHAPTER 3

Heaven Is Real

Heaven *is* real. When we begin to entertain heaven, when there is a free flow between heaven and earth, the manifestations that we see from the heavenly realms impact the terrestrial realms. It can take many different forms. I am speaking about becoming supernaturally syncopated or aligned fully with heaven today—in the now. It can be in the form of angelic ministry that releases signs and wonders. It can be in the form of supernatural provision, which many times is a dynamic of angelic ministry. In these instances God just begins to release supernatural grace and favor upon our lives for finances using His angels of creative miracles and supernatural provision (Psalm 103:20). These manifestations are beyond what normally occur in the natural realm and are supernaturally initiated. They do not make sense to our carnal minds. These kinds of manifestations of the Kingdom are spiritual in nature and are orchestrated by heaven. We just need to line up with heaven and believe to receive these types of supernatural blessings in our lives.

It is important to note that while there are supernatural manifestations that come from the Kingdom of God, there are also *preternatural* manifestations. *Preternatural paranormal manifestations proceed from and are derivatives of the occult* and New Age practices. Learn to discern the difference! One of my friends (who wishes to remain anonymous) teaches it like this:

> Super means above or beyond the natural realm. Preternatural mean alongside the natural. Therefore, super is a higher or superior realm. The first heaven is just the atmosphere around us. The second heaven is the preternatural realm (which includes the occult or the activity of the demonic realm). The third heaven is God's realm or abode and from that place or realm comes legitimate or the genuine supernatural. We should not seek to delve into the second heaven. Rather we actually need to access the third heaven realm.

Many theologians refer to the third heaven as the "heavenly places."

The Apostle Paul teaches us in 2 Corinthians, chapters 11 and 12, about the perils of false revelation and false teaching that originates in the preternatural realm. The lesson to learn (and I encourage you to diligently study 2 Corinthians chapters 11 and 12) is that you can get off track if you cannot discern revelation that emanates from the ungodly dimensions—specifically the second heaven. We need to learn to discern rightly, and this only comes as we learn to know the genuine nature of the Lord and the genuine and authentic heavenly places. Guard your heart! I hope that is clear.

Authentic Heavenly Places

We can begin to entertain heaven when we begin to cultivate our ability to enter into the heavenly realms (I'm talking about the glory of God, the presence of God). When we enter into that place of God's presence and we just rest there, there is a supernatural exchange that happens. When we invest enough time with God—God the Son, God the Father, and God the Holy Spirit—in the glory, that glory begins to rub off on us. God is a rewarder of those who are diligent to seek Him (Hebrews 11:6). Then we can learn to rightly release the *real* Kingdom of God wherever we go. Be advised; there are people who are releasing counterfeit signs and wonders today and those are *preternatural paranormal manifestations. The Scripture calls these kinds of counterfeit manifestations and experiences lying signs and wonders (2 Thessalonians 2:9).*

The True Children (Sons) of God

We don't have to fast and pray; we don't have to have a vision; we don't have to have a dream; we don't have to have a prophet call us out in a meeting and give us a prophetic word. We are just sons and daughters of God. Because when God's tangible presence (glory) rests upon you, then heaven is actually resting upon you. When this occurs it is the dynamic of Luke 11 and Matthew 6, as heaven comes upon the earth (in your life) as it is in heaven. You become supernaturally syncopated with heaven and God's grace and favor overtake you! One of my friends says Jesus outshines through you as you totally submit to Him and His Lordship in your life and surrender as an empty vessel of clay. Well, as for me (a boy from the mountains of West Virginia), "I'm Just an Old Chunk of Coal (But I'm Going to Be a Diamond Someday)," as the famous country music ballad proclaims![1]

There is a key worth repeating. John states it very clearly in 1 John 3:1:

> *Behold what manner of love the Father has bestowed on us, that we should be called children of God!*

We need the revelation that we are sons and daughters of the Father. The people on our team tell me why we cannot do something. I tell them, "Don't think like that. Think like your Father is a billionaire."

"But we don't have the money for...."

"Don't think like that; think like your Father is a billionaire and just begin to move towards that thing in the heavenly places of spiritual dimensions. Learn to call those things that are not as though they are" (Romans 4:17).

And do you know what begins to happen when you begin to think like your Father? (I'm not talking about your earthly father; I'm talking about your heavenly Father, Elohim.) Your heavenly Father is a multi-billionaire, and when you think from that perspective—"My Father is a billionaire"—when you begin to think and push that out of your spirit—"I don't care what it looks like in the natural, my Father is a billionaire"—supernatural things begin to happen. God begins to release supernatural grace and favor. And it comes from resting in His presence and in the glory. This supernatural dynamic (fresh manna) comes as you are diligent to meditate or study God's promises to you that are hidden in His word. These supernatural manifestations come from heaven and are released through God's supernatural grace and favor upon a believer's life.

The Inner Court

It's not necessarily about fasting, not necessarily about praying. It may not necessarily be about studying the word—although all those things are good and needful. But those are outer court exercises. Some people never grow past this stage. We need to learn to move past the outer court. We need to grow and mature in the Spirit. I'm talking about entering into and accessing the Holy of Holies and resting in His presence. I'm teaching you about entertaining heaven NOW!

Just abide in His presence and choose to make the secret place of the Most High your dwelling place (Psalm 91:1-2). This, by the way, is a conscious decision that you need to make every day! And when you do that, supernatural blessings begin to flow into your life from the Father's throne. The Father rewards you openly because you have sought Him in the secret place (Matthew 6:18). There is a supernatural exchange that takes place. And your Father begins to smile upon you; plus the Lord purposefully and intentionally places grace and favor upon you. It is not by works; it comes by relationship. The Father might think or say, "Look at that. That's one of My children! I know what they have need of even before they ask" (Matthew 6:8). Sometimes as you learn to entertain heaven God will answer your prayers even before the words leave your lips! Selah!

We just begin to decree that in our thoughts and speak these things out loud with our words and declarations: "I will prosper and be in health even as my soul prospers." And God begins to move the mountains in our life to make these desires of our hearts possible. The Father places a grace upon our prayer life.

You could say that we grow in favor with both God and man and the Lord places a "mantle of prayer" upon our life. Really, this is just learning to discern heavenly places correctly and walk in them. As a result, the directives of the Lord and the heart of heaven are poured into our lives (manifest) here on earth! Learn to discern what is of God and what is counterfeit. Learn to tell the difference between the third heaven and the second heaven, the supernatural and the preternatural, the holy and the profane, the good and the evil. This supernatural discernment is imperative! The good news is that it is freely given to you from your heavenly Father. Just ask Him for it!

Grab the Altar by the Horns!

Really what I am talking about is entertaining the heavenly realms. You can learn to entertain heaven. As you read this book, you will have a wonderful opportunity to receive impartation and activation. Even just reading about God releasing miracles, signs, and wonders can create an atmosphere where you can grab the supernatural nature of heaven and the miraculous character of Christ for yourself. You don't really need someone to lay hands on you. You can just receive God's heavenly blessings by being in the atmosphere and glory of God. Speak it out loud with your personal word declarations! Pray the Scriptures audibly over your life and circumstances every day. Learn to move heaven to earth in your life and circumstances! You can activate this supernatural dynamic by simply reading this book and making a conscious decision to believe what you read is from the heart of God for your life and circumstances! What do you have to lose? Your sickness, your poverty, your hopelessness and despair! Go for it! Grab the altar by the horns of the altar! Develop a lifestyle of taking the Kingdom of God by violence and force each and every day (Matthew 11:12). Become a radical believer!

When you begin to entertain heaven and you begin to invest time waiting upon the Lord in the heavenly places, the atmosphere of heaven begins to rub off on you. At times the terrestrial realm or the earthly realm and the heavenly realm are superimposed over one another. So it is not so much that we have to go "up" to heaven—although I share several third heaven testimonies of the times the Lord has allowed me to actually visit the heavenly places. But we can learn to discern the heavenly reality and grow to know that heaven is all around us right now; even as you are reading this book. Take a minute and think about that! You don't have to go up to heaven, just access the heavenly places all around you right now by faith!

The Father Does the Works

Then we begin to decree and call those things that are not as though they are according to Romans 4:17 (for example decreeing that someone is receiving gold crowns on their teeth or someone is supernaturally losing weight instantly, as they just believed what was decreed). We just decree those things and the heavenly realm begins to manifest in the natural realm. We have seen the Lord release hundreds of dental miracles like this. I discern or entertain heaven before I step into our meetings to minister and release the heavenly revelation and directives the Lord reveals to me in prayer upon the earth. We move vertically into heaven to receive revelation and then release that revelation horizontally on the earth. It is a picture of the Cross of Calvary. Jesus ministered the same way; He entertained heaven. Remember Jesus taught us in John 5:19: *"Most assuredly, I say to you, the Son can do nothing of Himself, but what He sees the Father do; for whatever He does, the Son also does in like manner."*

The Lord also spoke of this dynamic of entertaining heaven in John 5:30: *"I can of Myself do nothing. As I hear, I judge; and My judgment is righteous, because I do not seek My own will but the will of the Father who sent Me."* The Lord also stated in John 14:10: *"Do you not believe that I am in the Father, and the Father in Me? The words that I speak to you I do not speak on My own authority; but the Father who dwells in Me does the works."* Jesus was speaking about the attesting signs in His ministry. He was speaking about the miracles, signs, and wonders that followed Him everywhere. The Lord is teaching us that He accessed (entertained) heaven to see what His Father was doing and then just did what He saw the Father doing. Well, if the Father is in heaven (and we know He is), then Jesus is giving us keys to entertaining heaven. Again, this is a picture of the Cross of Calvary. You ascend vertically into the heavens to see what the Father is doing (entertain heaven), then you release or imitate horizontally upon the earth the revelations that you "see" or discern.

Your Spirit Man

Does it make sense in the natural? No! Remember, we learned from 1 Corinthians, chapter 2, that heaven and spiritual truth are not discerned through your carnal mind but are spiritually discerned. So you need to massage your spirit man. How do you do that? You massage your spirit man by spending time in the glory of God; investing time in a place where the atmosphere of heaven is present, where the atmosphere of heaven invades; investing time around people who are heavenly minded; investing time around people who can speak and give you insights, wisdom, and revelation from their legitimate personal experiences in the heavenly realms. Of course, you can read all of the heavenly encounters from the pages of your Bible too. Learn of these supernatural encounters like John's vision of heaven from Revelation 4 or Ezekiel's heavenly vision in Ezekiel 1, to suggest a couple. Study the visionaries of the Bible consistently as you move to develop your spiritual senses.

Look for people who consistently access the *real* glory of God and align yourself with them (not imitators). Receive them and receive your reward. You massage your spirit man by learning from other people's experiences and messages. You can receive from their audio teachings and books. When you are in those places and in those times when you are around such people who carry the Kingdom of Heaven, there's impartation being poured out. Sometimes you just have to catch it! The anointing is often better caught than taught! The Holy Spirit will give you a witness in your spirit when you come to a place and ministry that He wants you to glean from. You can "*raah*" it, you can discern it. On the other hand the Spirit can also give you a check when there is a counterfeit anointing in operation. If you get a check in your spirit, you should question the content of the message, book, or other resource or just leave the service.

I know many brothers and sisters who teach about the glory and they teach about miracles and they teach about signs and wonders, but you don't see a lot of them in their ministry. You see, they have head knowledge of it, and that's great; but you need to have an experience with heaven. We can teach you about heaven from the Scripture, but you need to have an encounter with heaven. You need to have a witness of the Holy Spirit concerning manifestations of the glory, the gifts of the Spirit, and signs and wonders these days. Learn to discern what is real from what is false; what is of the Holy Spirit and what is of the flesh—that is hype (2 Corinthians 11:13-15).

I know many people who have had a legitimate encounter with heaven and it changed their lives forever. They are always drawn closer to Jesus and begin to live for Him alone when they encounter heaven. You can have an encounter with heaven as you read this book. Why do I say that? It's because the testimony of Jesus is the spirit of prophecy (Revelation 19:10). Nearly every time we have had a school or a teaching on this subject, there have been people who have had visitations with the Lord Jesus Christ or they have had a visionary glimpse of heaven. They have experienced a personal open-eyed encounter where Jesus literally appeared to them! Would you like that? Entertain heaven, lean into it. What's it going to look like for you? I don't know. Just purpose in your heart and ask the Lord for help: "I want that, Lord. Lord, please activate my spiritual discernment as I read this book and seek Your face!"

In the next chapter we will take a hermeneutical look at the heavens in the Scripture as we continue to build a foundation on entertaining heaven. If Jesus did it, you can do it. Heaven is real. Heaven is unfolding around you right now!

CHAPTER 4

Heavenly Dimensions

Let's investigate what the Scripture actually teaches us about heaven in more detail. Let's look at the first mention of heaven in the Bible. We find it in Genesis 1. Using these scriptures let's build a more sure foundation in our biblical understanding about heaven. Allow me to take a hermeneutical approach to heaven here. Genesis 1:1 says, *"In the beginning God created the heavens and the earth."* The very first scripture in the Bible tells us God created the heavens. The word used for heaven here is plural—heaven(s). Many translations of the Bible use the plural form of heaven when rendering Genesis 1:1. Scripture is clear in that there are numerous places in the realms of heaven.

Going on with verses 2-3, it says, *"The earth was without form, and void; and darkness was on the face of the deep. And the Spirit of God was hovering over the face of the waters. Then God said, 'Let there be light'; and there was light."* In verse 4 we read, *"And God saw the light..."* The Hebrew word translated "saw" here is the root word for seer. What I would like for you to grasp here is that God created light after He created the heavens and the earth. Why do we need light? We need light so we can see. What is Jesus? He *is* the light (John 8:12).

So there is a type of sight that has been given to us (the creature by the Creator), the supernatural sight we were learning about earlier in Ephesians 1, 1 Corinthians 2, and 1 John 3. There is a supernatural sight that comes where we begin to emulate the Lord's model and we begin to see in a supernatural way. We see differently and look differently. We hear differently and comprehend differently. Jesus touched on this in Luke 8:18: *"Therefore take heed how you hear."* The Lord indicated that there is more than one way to see and hear. We begin to see spiritually; we begin to discern spiritually. We begin to see and discern in a new and supernatural way. Going on in Genesis 1 with verses 4 and 5, we read,

> *And God saw the light, that it was good; and God divided the light from the darkness. God called the light Day, and the darkness He called Night. So the evening and the morning were the first day.*

God then made a firmament. We read in verse 8, *"And God called the firmament Heaven,"* speaking of the celestial realm. *"So the evening and the morning were the second day."*

In verse 9 the word of God continues: *"Then God said, 'Let the waters under the heavens be gathered together into one place, and let the dry land appear'; and it was so."* So, of course, this is the biblical description of Creation. We see that God created the heavens or the heavenly realms (multiple places). He created a celestial realm and He created a terrestrial realm—the heavens and the earth. Again, note that "heavens" is plural. In verse 14 we read (emphasis added):

> *Then God said, "Let there be lights in the firmament of the heavens* [plural] *to divide the day from the night; and let them be for signs and* **seasons [*moed*, appointed time]**, *and for days and years."*

Going on in verses 16-18, it says,

> *Then God made two great lights: the greater light to rule the day, and the lesser light to rule the night. He made the stars also. God set them in the firmament of the heavens* [plural] *to give light on the earth, and to rule over the day and over the night, and to divide the light from the darkness. And God saw that it was good.*

Further on we see that God creates creatures both on the land and in the sea. And He said that it was good and He blessed them. In verses 24 and 25, we read,

> *Then God said, "Let the earth bring forth the living creature according to its kind: cattle and creeping thing and beast of the earth, each according to its kind"; and it was so. And God made the beast of the earth according to its kind, cattle according to its kind, and everything that creeps on the earth according to its kind. And God saw that it was good.*

Now verse 26 is where it gets really interesting: "*Then God said, 'Let Us make man in Our image, according to Our likeness...'.*" Then we see in verses 27 and 28 it says, "*So God created man in His own image; in the image of God He created him; male and female He created them. Then God blessed them, and God said to* them, *'Be fruitful and multiply....'"* In verse 29, God said, *"See..."* He's speaking to His creation. When the Creator speaks to the creature and says, "See" (*raah*), He's telling us to see in more than one way.

Raah is a Hebrew word (Strong's Hebrew Concordance H7200) that can be translated "to discern." *Raah* is a primitive root that can mean to see, literally or figuratively, to appear, approve, behold, certainly, consider, discern, (make to) enjoy, to have an experience, to gaze, to take heed, to look (on, one another, one on another, one upon another, to look out, up, upon), to mark, to meet, to be near, to perceive, to regard with respect, to be shown, to spy, to stare, to think or to view, to behold visions.

Here is my definition of *raah*, which is scripturally associated with the seer function or seer operation: To have your supernatural senses activated to discern or see heavenly revelation and to discern or know and understand the heart of God for your life by accessing heavenly revelation.

In the Beginning

You see, we were created in God's image. We were created with the ability and gift to see (*raah*). God created us to see and discern or "*raah*" between the heavenly realms and the terrestrial realm. But what has happened over the course of time, because of the Fall, is that our human nature has inhibited us from having spiritual discernment like we saw in 1 Corinthians, chapter 2. We no longer discern heavenly things. But I've got good news for you! We can discern heavenly things or spiritual truth with the help of the Holy Spirit and with our own mature and sanctified spirit. We can begin to see and discern heavenly things. We can begin to understand heavenly realities. God is going to begin to open up spiritual ears and eyes so that you will be enabled or activated to discern revelation from the Gospel that you read. Again, I call this entertaining heaven.

Of course, Jesus Christ was there in the beginning or at Creation. It was the Lord (the Word) who was present when the heavens were created. The Gospel of John clarifies this biblical truth in chapter 1, verses 1-5:

> *In the beginning was the Word, and the Word was with God, and the Word was God. He was in the beginning with God. All things were made through Him, and without Him nothing was made that was made. In Him was life, and the life was the light of men. And the light shines in the darkness, and the darkness did not comprehend it.*

So we are created in God's image and God created the heavenly realms, multiple heavens. God created multiple heavenly places or heavenly realms for you to discern, see, interact with, and/or become aware of. I want to stop a minute and study what Paul said in the first few verses of 2 Corinthians 12 about knowing a man who was caught up into the third heaven and paradise. People want to talk about how many realms of heaven there are. Who cares? The bottom line is that there are multiple realms of heaven. Here are some interesting thoughts for discussion and to ponder:

There are a few scientists who believe that they have discovered parallel dimensions or parallel universes around each of us right now at this second (this is quantum psychics). So my question to you becomes: are these dimensions (parallel dimensions or parallel universes) or have they discovered heavenly places? Perhaps they are; perhaps they are not. This is debatable and at this as point they are theory only. These hypotheses are not proven or established scientifically. You see, some scientists propose that objects (you and me as the creature, human beings) are actually blinking in and out of existence about a thousand times per second, or something like that. One nanosecond we are here; then, poof, the next nanosecond we are gone. They don't know where we go; they theorize that we are just not in this dimension. So, if this is true, where are we going? The inference is into a dual or parallel dimension for a nanosecond. Perhaps it is possible that we are oscillating back and forth between two dimensions. You could easily speak of these two places as the temporal realm and the heavenly realms.

Visionary Heavenly Encounters

It is possible that we are accessing the heavenly places or heavenly dimensions without being aware of it. Why and how? Because that is what our God given-spiritual DNA consists of. Again, this is speculation. However, when we die, it is our spirit that will be transported into the realms of heaven. So it is possible that some scientists have accidentally stumbled upon actual evidence of the existence of heaven. Again, this is conjecture on my part, but it is intriguing! Also, allow me to say that the testimonies that I have included later in this book are most likely visions of heaven or the heavenly places (heavenly encounters). To state this concisely, I do not believe that

I went to heaven in my body but rather that I had a visionary experience where my spirit man was caught up to heaven. (I have come to believe this since these experiences transpired about eighteen years ago as of this writing.)

Let's go back and focus on Genesis, chapter 2, verse 1: *"Thus the heavens and the earth, and all the host of them, were finished."* Think about that, the heavens (plural). How many did God make? I'm not sure; multitudes. I believe there are innumerable dimensions and innumerable realms of heaven. I'm not going to debate about it; I don't want to get into a theological debate or apologetics about how many realms of heaven exist. That is a waste of precious time. One day when you are with Jesus in heaven, you can ask Him. Okay? I'm just telling you that there are more dimensions to heaven or more heavenly places than we understand with our limited human knowledge and reasoning or carnal mind (1 Corinthians 2:14). God is vast and so are the heavenly places and all the realms of heaven that the Lord created! Just think, you will get to explore all of those heavenly places one day!

What's exciting about this supernatural dynamic is we have eternity to explore all of the heavenly places that God created for you. Hallelujah! What do you think we are going to do in heaven? We are not going to be in just one place in heaven. You will be free to (ding ding) "move about the cabin" in heaven. You can move about the heavenly realms. Sometimes God reveals to me various geographical places in the heavenly places. Again, these supernatural experiences are most likely visions that have been initiated by the Spirit of God. The Spirit of God will take me into the heavenly places, and I observe (seer operation) the heavenly realms. God had allowed me to tour various heavenly places in these visions. There are multitudes of places in heaven, and that's your inheritance. You have a home prepared for you in heaven (John 14:2).

But what I want you to understand is that you don't have to die to entertain heaven. You can entertain heaven today, right now. And as you learn to entertain heaven, it can transform your life. But it's not something you are going to be able to figure out with your carnal mind because it's a spiritual dynamic. Just by reading this book and investing your time to entertain the heavenly realms, or the glory realms, there is a supernatural transaction that happens and the realms of heaven will rub off on you. And you begin to walk in a supernatural lifestyle. It's fun! It is available. It's free, but it is not inexpensive. You must pick up your cross and follow Jesus—dying to yourself daily.

I want to convey and review a couple of scriptures we've touched on already. These have merit in this hermeneutical look at heaven. Again, we are talking about entertaining the heavenly realms. In Ephesians, chapter 1, verse 3, in the Montgomery translation[1] it says we have been blessed with *"every spiritual blessing in the **heavenly realms** in Christ"* (emphasis added). In the New King James translation, it calls it *"heavenly places."* It's the same thing. We could call those created spaces heavenly dimensions, especially if you are not churchy and starchy—I'm just sayin'.

Let's go to the Book of Ephesians, chapter 3. (By the way, these are like my life's verses here. I bow my knees and I pray this prayer most every day. Some days I pray it two or three times a day. Some days I miss it, but I encourage you to pray this prayer consistently—first thing in the morning, in the afternoon, at night—whenever you can.) Starting with verses 14 through 16, we read,

> *For this reason I bow my knees to the Father of our Lord Jesus Christ, from whom the whole family in heaven and earth is named, that He would grant you, according to the riches of His glory, to be strengthened with might through His Spirit in the inner man.*

What this means is that God (the Creator) would grant to you or ministers to you (the creature) supernatural grace or power. Did you know God wants to minister to you supernatural grace or power to transform you into the image of Jesus? You don't have to do it yourself. You have a heavenly Father who can initiate and help you with your spiritual transformation and your revelations of heaven.

Going on with verse 17: *"That Christ may dwell in your hearts through faith; that you, being rooted and grounded in love."* How? In love! Verse 18 continues the prayer that you *"may be able to comprehend with all the saints what is the width and length and depth and height."* These are all what I call Godly dimensions. These are aspects or realms of the heavenly places.

And what happens when you access the heavenly places? Verse 19 says you begin *"to know the love of Christ which passes knowledge; that you may be filled with all the fullness of God."* This is a Hebraism that means we might be filled with the divinity or the nature of God, Elohim. You could say that you mature in your faith and grow to supernaturally develop the mind of Christ within you to replace your carnal mindset.

In other words, you become heavenly minded or a heavenly man or woman. Imagine that! It is possible for you to be transformed by the Spirit of God right now! Just say, "Yes, Lord," to that and believe to receive it as you meditate upon the King and His Kingdom as you read this book!

CHAPTER 5

Heavenly Perspectives

Do you want to be filled with the divinity or nature of Elohim? You see, when we become filled with the nature of God, then we begin to have that spiritual discernment that we saw in 1 Corinthians 2, verse 9, activated in our lives: *"But as it is written: 'Eye has not seen, nor ear heard, Nor have entered into the heart of man The things which God has prepared for those who love Him.'"*

That's what Jesus did. Jesus had a different concept about life and about ministry. Jesus did not look at circumstances the way we look at circumstances. They came to Jesus and said, "Lord, your taxes are due." Jesus thought, "Ah! This is an opportunity for My God and Father to do something amazing!" He told them, "Go fishing. And the first fish you catch will have enough money in its mouth to pay the taxes." (See Matthew 17:27.) Does that make sense in the natural? No! It is a supernatural exchange.

Heavenly Perspective

When our spiritual discernment is activated and flowing, then we no longer see things from our limited earthly perspective; we see things from a heavenly perspective. I want to see things the way my Father sees them. This is an operation of the seer anointing. We need to overcome our small mindedness and/or petty mindsets.

That's the way I want to think. You see, God can give us supernatural wisdom and revelation that is not carnal; God can give us supernatural wisdom and revelation that is not earthly but that is mighty in God. This supernatural wisdom and revelation develops gradually (most times) in our lives as we become transformed into the image of Jesus. As a result our spiritual discernment is activated so that we can entertain, understand, or discern heavenly things. (For example, how Jesus paid His taxes.) This does not happen overnight. It happens over the course of time. It is a supernatural learning curve, so don't get frustrated. Just keep trusting your heavenly Father to give you His good gifts (James 1:17). God can also drop wisdom and revelation upon you as He wills. Now that is a perfect gift!

I know folks who have come to our meetings over the past several years whose lives are transformed; not so much because hands have been laid upon them or not so much because of the preaching, but because they have come into the atmosphere where heaven is invading earth. They access the presence of the Lord and the glory of God in our gatherings. They've come into the atmosphere where the heavenly realms are manifesting—where miracles, signs, and wonders are taking place. People like this have their lives transformed because the way that they think is renewed by the presence and the Spirit of the living God. They see the reality of the Kingdom of Heaven modeled and realize that they can walk in the Kingdom too just as it has been demonstrated before them.

They no longer struggle with poverty, they no longer struggle with oppression, and they no longer struggle with sickness. There's just a supernatural exchange that takes place. It is not hype! The Kingdom of Heaven comes and Heaven Touches Earth! In other words, what I'm saying is that sometimes in the heavenly realms, in the anointing, in the glory, the Kingdom of God is better caught than taught. In the atmosphere of heaven, God can transform your mind into the mind of Christ (1 Corinthians 2:16).

Above All

Let's look at this dynamic again in Ephesians 3:19 where Paul is praying that you may be able *"to know the love of Christ which passes knowledge; that you may be filled with all the fullness of God."* Let it be so! It ends with verses 20 and 21: *"Now to Him who is able to do exceedingly abundantly above all that we ask or think, according to the power that works in us, to Him be glory in the church by Christ Jesus to all generations, forever and ever. Amen."* What's the key? **Him**—our Father who is in heaven—*"who is able to [carry out His purpose and] do superabundantly more than all that we dare ask or think [infinitely beyond our greatest prayers, hopes, or dreams]"* (Ephesians 3:20, AMP).

You see, we need to change the way we think. We need to change the way we think about heaven. Heaven is not necessarily "up there" (though it is); heaven is all around us. Heaven is not necessarily a destination that we are going to go to when we die and we put off this body (earth suit). The Scripture says to be absent from the body is to be present with the Lord (2

Corinthians 5:8). Heaven is all around us right now. The issue is we don't discern it. Our spiritual discernment may have grown dull or may not have been developed fully.

But occasionally we come to a place, a point in time, a *moed*, an appointed season, an eternal crossroads on God's calendar where the heavens open. God has already preordained for us to access heaven today. It's not going to be hard. It's not going to be difficult. You can learn to discern the heavenly realms in your life NOW. You don't necessarily have to go up to access heaven because heaven is all around you right now! You can live under an open heaven, but first you must learn to discern an open heaven.

There are people all over the world who are having encounters with heaven. By the grace of God through the power of the Holy Spirit (because of God's grace upon my life) and by having the ability to write a few books about heaven and angels and the seer anointing, we get testimonies and emails all the time from people all over the world. These people are accessing the reality of heaven or entertaining heaven without trying. "Jesus stepped into my bedroom." "I saw an angel in my car. When the angel was in my car a truck ran a red light and passed straight through my car and didn't touch it and there was no damage! I should have been killed but somehow the truck didn't even touch the car."

We get these types of testimonies all the time. Why is that? Because the veil between heaven and earth is thin; it's transparent; it's more porous than any time in history. And you can enter into heaven too. It's not about being a pastor or a teacher or a prophet or an evangelist or an apostle, as wonderful as those things are. It's about being a son or daughter of the Most High God. God wants to pour out His Spirit upon His children. Last I checked the Lord said that He would *"pour out of My Spirit on all flesh"* (Acts 2:17)! I believe we are at a point in time when the realms of heaven are going to be poured out in such a powerful way that it will not be deniable. It's going to be seen on mainline television. There will be no way to explain what happens. We don't know why this happens, but it must be something supernatural. I'll tell you what the supernatural is; it's Jesus, it's the God of Israel, it's Elohim, it's God the Father pouring out His Kingdom upon the earth. Watch for amazing testimonies of God intervening in the nation of Israel in the coming years. These supernatural interventions will be seen on international network television news programming. In fact, it has already happened! Now let's learn about two differing mindsets and concepts concerning the reality of heaven. Are you ready?

CHAPTER 6

Discerning Heavenly Places

Let me talk to you a little bit more about heaven. We looked at it in Genesis. In the Old Testament the word that is translated "heaven" is the Hebrew word *shamayim*, which has a dual meaning. It means a lofty place or it means the sky, referring to the visible arch above the earth *or* a higher realm where celestial bodies reside. So there is a heavenly place in the natural realm where there are celestial bodies. We studied this it in Genesis 1:14, where God appointed signs in the sky, like the sun and the moon for seasons or appointed times.

But there is also another place in the spiritual realm that we call the heavenly places and Scripture also refers to them as the heavenly places. So the Hebrew word translated "heaven" is different than the word translated "heaven" we see in the New Testament. Most of the time the word translated for "heaven" in the New Testament is the Greek word *ouranos*. It means the sky or heaven, the abode of God, or by implication eternity—a heavenly place specifically in relation to Christianity and Jesus Christ. Do you want to go there?

There are heavenly places (or dimensions such as the second heaven) that are not Godly; I call those ungodly dimensions. Some of us are oppressed because there are ungodly doors open in our lives through generational issues that we have nothing to do with. I am a Cherokee Indian, and I am an

Italian. So there were spiritual doors open in my life to nefarious things; for example: witchcraft, drug abuse, and I could go on and on. But by the grace of God, through the power of the Holy Spirit, and through blood of Jesus and the cleansing work and atonement of Jesus Christ on the Cross of Calvary, I was set free. God can close those doors into ungodly dimensions over your life and break generational curses and iniquities off of your life and your family line too. This will result in an immediate change (for the better) in your life.

As you read this some of you will be delivered and you are going to be set free of oppressive things and generational issues through activation. Activation can be about receiving something but it can also be about something being blocked or something being closed that allows the enemy access to oppress you. Do you want to be set free? Do you want to be set free from the inability to hear God well? Do you want to be set free from poverty? Do you want to be set free from sickness? Do you want to be set free from generational issues like arthritis, diabetes, chronic back pain, and other debilitating diseases and things like that?

It can happen. This is an aspect of entertaining heaven. When we access the heavenly places, there are times that God can release supernatural healing and deliverance into our lives that can totally transform us. Why? Because that is the day and the hour we live in.

Holy and the Profane

Let's look at the Book of Colossians. I like Colossians. In chapter 1 we continue to see the story of Creation unfold in the

Scriptures. These passages are talking about God who created the earthly realm and the heavenly realms and the host of heaven. There are a lot of spiritual beings that inhabit the heavenly places; not all of them are good. We need to be able to discern the difference between the holy and the profane or unholy, the Godly and the ungodly (Ezekiel 44:23). As you read the teaching in this chapter, God is going to release to many of you the Spirit of wisdom and revelation and the gift of discerning of spirits.

Let's begin in Colossians 1:16:

For by Him all things were created that are in heaven and that are on earth, visible and invisible, whether thrones or dominions or principalities or powers. All things were created through Him and for Him.

So, all the things in heavenly places were created by God for His purposes. Obviously a disconnect happened; it's called the Fall of man. Many people have many different theologies and ideas about this; but what I want you to see is that in the heavenly realms (which are multiple, there are multitudes of heavenly realms), there are many spiritual beings and not all of them are good. But through the finished work of Jesus Christ on the Cross of Calvary, He has given us power and authority over those fallen things (demons), as we understand who we are in Christ.

In my book *Unlocking the Hidden Mysteries of the Age to Come*, I share a little bit about the history of Moravian Falls and about how people go there seeking spiritual experiences. I also talk about how there are spiritual gates open in that geographic area and region. Many of these were spiritual gates were opened by the original inhabitants of the land, the Cherokees Indians. Of course, I am using Moravian Falls as an example. It is important to understand that not all of the spiritual gates around Moravian Falls open into Godly dimensions. The same dynamic is true for other geographic areas, like Sedona, Arizona, Jerusalem, and others too. You need to develop your spiritual discernment. You could call this geographical discernment.

Some of the gates in geographic places open up into the second heaven or demonic dimensions and places. Some people who come to Moravian Falls seeking a spiritual experience with little or no discernment get what I call "slimed." Because of their spiritual blindness they get spiritually defiled. Their zeal leads them into unholy experiences and they aren't able to discern the difference in what is holy and what is profane or evil.

So if you are seeking to entertain heaven, this is a clear and clarion call and warning. "Danger, Will Robinson!" You must be careful; because if you are seeking a spiritual experience and you are immature and you are not in the place you need to be with God—in other words you are not walking in righteousness and holiness, you have not submitted to the cleansing fire of the Holy Spirit, you allow sin to reign in your mortal body—and you begin to press into this aspect of God's Kingdom, you can get spiritually defiled. Without mature discernment people can get sick; some people may even die from becoming defiled spiritually. So be aware of that. What we are talking about is a very serious issue. You should not try to entertain heaven without being prepared spiritually.

We can access heaven; we can enter into the heavenly realms because of the finished work of Jesus Christ. We can access the heavenly places in total safety. We are living in the day and hour of acceleration before the coming and return of the Lord Jesus Christ. The dynamics of Revelation 4, verse 1, are manifesting in people's lives at this time:

> *After these things I looked, and behold, a door standing open in heaven. And the first voice which I heard was like a trumpet speaking with me, saying, "Come up here, and I will show you things which must take place after this."*

Later on in verse 11 it says:

> *You are worthy, O Lord, To receive glory and honor and power; For You created all things, And by Your will they exist and were created.*

Scripture clearly indicates that all the heavenly things were created by God for His purposes. We're going to entertain heaven, and everything we are going to entertain was created by God. Some of those things, though, have fallen and are no longer righteous or holy. So, we need to be aware of that. We need great spiritual discernment at this hour. We can pass through the heavens and entertain the heavenly realms. And again, it's not necessarily that we go up to do that. Sometimes we can do that by simply discerning heavenly truth or heavenly realms and spiritual dynamics that are unfolding all around us on the earth. Sometimes these spiritual dynamics are evil and profane, so you need to learn to discern that.

The Finished Work of Jesus

Let's continue to study this dynamic in the Book of Hebrews, chapter 4, for a moment. Let's talk about why we can do that. My job is to build a foundation for you. The reason we can access the heavenly places is because of the finished work of Jesus Christ. It all has to do with the rest of the Lord. Hebrews, chapter 4, is all about entering into, being diligent to enter into the rest of the Lord. Do you know what that is? It's the glory of God, the presence of God, the Kingdom of God. The rest of the Lord is simply accessing and discerning the attributes and truths of heaven while we are alive upon the earth. We learn to trust in Him completely as we discern the reality of His will for our lives.

Let's look at verse 11: *"Let us therefore be diligent to enter that rest, lest anyone fall according to the same example of disobedience."* Now this passage of Scripture, of course, is referring to the children of Israel when they were in the desert. But it is parabolic of us today too.

His Might

There is a place of rest in God's Kingdom for us; and that place of rest has everything we need for a joyous and prosperous life in Christ.

When we seek the Father in the secret place He awards us openly. In that place of rest, there is a supernatural exchange that can take place where God can take us from poverty to prosperity; He can take us from sickness to health; He can take us from hopelessness to hope. And when we begin to enter that place—when we are diligent to enter into the rest of the Lord, the presence, the glory of God, the holy of holies—in that place

God begins to move on our behalf. How? We read of it in Zechariah 4:6. But it is summed up here in Hebrews 4:14: *"Seeing then that we have a great High Priest who has passed through the heavens, Jesus the Son of God, let us hold fast our confession."*

We are called to be the royal priesthood according to the order of Melchizedek. In other words, we are called to re-create Jesus in our sphere of influence. And if Jesus passed through the heavens, we too are called to pass through the heavens. Zechariah 4:6 also illustrates this heavenly principle: *"So he answered and said to me: 'This is the word of the LORD to Zerubbabel: "Not by might nor by power, but by My Spirit," Says the LORD of hosts.'"* When we learn to discern the directives of the Holy Spirit in our lives there is a supernatural transfer of the power of heaven into our lives and circumstances.

We rest and the Spirit of God works upon our behalf. We do not have to work with our human reasoning, physical strength, or apply our wealth to a situation. The power of the Holy Spirit supernaturally moves upon our behalf. Again, I will use the testimony of the Holy Spirit directing me to pray for new homes in 2001. At that point in time I was poor and in the natural and it would be impossible for me to purchase even one new home.

However, I became obedient and prayed in agreement with the heavenly pattern that the Spirit of the Lord revealed to me through revelation or entertaining heaven. I positioned myself to become supernaturally syncopated with heaven in intercession. Today, seventeen years later as of this writing, the Lord has supernaturally led my steps and (by God's grace) I have had four new homes since this epiphany, and orchestrated building seven other homes for orphans. That is the supernatural grace of resting in the Lord. There is a divine exchange and Jesus turns your dimes into dollars and the grace and favor of the Lord begins to rest upon you and God will bless all of the works of your hands and you begin to supernaturally prosper (Deuteronomy 28:12).

Melchizedek

Look at Hebrews, chapter 5, verse 9. It says, *"And having been perfected, He became the author of eternal salvation to all who obey Him."* Have you prayed to receive Jesus Christ, Yeshua Hamashiach, as your Savior and Messiah? If you have, God has a destiny for you. You can see it in verse 10 where we read we are called royal priests by God *"according to the order of Melchizedek."* (See also 1 Peter 2:9.) What does that mean? It means that you taste of the good words and the powers of the age to come (Hebrews 6:5). One important aspect of these powers of the age to come that I have sought to focus on in this book is answered prayer. Leaning to become triumphant in prayer unlocks the powers of the age to come in your life and in your sphere of influence. Becoming triumphant in prayer inevitably will supernaturally transform your life and circumstances. It means there is an immutable promise that God determined to show to us abundantly, the heirs of salvation, that He confirmed by an oath (v. 17). Verse 18 assures us that it is impossible for God to lie and that we have a refuge to take hold of. What is that refuge? We have a High Priest, Jesus Christ, according to the order of Melchizedek (v. 20), who has passed behind the veil or through the heavens.

We have that same destiny. We can pass through the heavens. We can entertain the heavenly realms just as Jesus did. It's not some hyper-spiritual thing; it's not some far-fetched theology. Jesus said, *"The works that I do [you] will do"* (John 14:12). If Jesus passed through the heavens, guess what? We can pass through the heavens too. How do we do that? We do it the same way Jesus did.

The Eternal Key

The key to entertaining the heavenly realms is the blood of God. The key to entertaining the heavenly realms is the finished work of Jesus Christ on the Cross of Calvary. Any other access into the spiritual realm is trespassing. The only legal means to access the heavenly places is Christ Jesus. It's only through the finished work of Jesus Christ on the Cross that we can entertain or access the heavenly realms.

Here is another brief testimony about entertaining heaven to receive revelation that manifests in your life to transform who you are in Christ. As a new believer I had these incredible supernatural experiences in Canada in 2001. God opened up my eyes and I began to see angels. All the time, everywhere I went for months, I saw angels. One day the Lord allowed me to be taken up into heaven with Jesus, and He said, "Kevin, you need to get a computer and write all of these things down."

I said, "Lord, I don't have a computer. I don't know where to get a computer."

And in heaven the Lord spoke to me and said, "There's a man named Bobby who will be in church on Sunday. When you go to church on Sunday, tell Bobby you need a computer."

Accessing the heavenly places like this sounds pretty easy, doesn't it? Sunday came along, I went to church, and sure enough, there's Bobby. I couldn't get courage enough to go to him and say, "Hey, Bobby, I was in heaven and Jesus said you would give me a computer." So I just bit my tongue and thought, "If I'm supposed to talk to Bobby, Bobby will come and talk to me." Well, he never did.

I left church and was being beaten up by the enemy because I was disobedient to God and what the Lord told me to do in heavenly places. I said, "O Jesus! I am so sorry! I promise I will listen to You and obey you next time You show me what to do, I promise!"

Teachable moment: In the heavenly realms when God gives you an assignment, when He speaks to you and tells you to do something, obedience is critical; it is key. You must be immediately obedient.

So I said, "Lord, if I see Bobby again next Sunday or the next time I see Bobby, I promise You I'm going to tell him about that computer."

So, I stopped to get gas. Guess who was at the gas pump? Bobby! I drew him aside. I didn't say I was talking to Jesus in heaven, but I said, "Hey, Bobby, do you think that you could get me a computer? I think I need a computer." This was basically what the Lord had instructed me in the heavenly places to say to Bobby. It is important to listen carefully and repeat verbatim exactly what you hear in circumstances like these.

He said, "Come by my house about six o'clock." I went by Bobby's house that same night. Within twenty-four hours that computer was sitting on my kitchen table. With God all things are possible to those who believe.

CHAPTER 7

Heavenly Revelation and Earthly Manifestation

So I would go to heaven and visit these amazing places with Jesus. I would come back and I would write it all down because Jesus had told me to "write the things that you see and hear." So now that I had this old beaten up computer, I did. I would write down everything that I experienced whilst I was in the presence of Jesus in the heavenly places. When that old computer crashed, I took the hard drive from it and kept it for some reason. Ten years later I was visiting the Lord in heaven again when Lord spoke to me and said, "Kevin, do you remember all those things you wrote down when I got you that PC?"

I said, "Yea."

He said, "Get them. It's going to be a book. It will be your bestselling book."

So I took that old hard drive and got a very nice friend, Bob Spruill, to help me to pull the information and writings off of the old hard drive. I took all of those writings; and with the help of the Holy Spirit I polished them into a book, and that's how *Angels in Realms of Heaven* came to pass. That book was sold in Walmart all over America for a season. My pastor purchased a copy for me from Walmart! It was sold all over the world. People started to call me and tell me that my book was being sold in Walmart! And guess what? It was the most successful book of them all until 2014.

When we entertain heaven we will often be given heavenly patterns. If we are obedient to place our hands to the heavenly plans that God gives to us, the grace and favor of God will be upon the works of our hands. As you learn to become supernaturally syncopated with heaven and obedient in your prayer life, the Lord begins to release the resources of heaven to work on your behalf. Heavenly revelation then can be transformed into reality and takes the form of earthly manifestation.

That's a testimony and an example of how you can entertain heaven and there can be a supernatural manifestation on the earth. I could tell you countless dozens of testimonies like that. For Kathy, my wife, and me, it is just a lifestyle.

O Canada

I was telling you about being in Canada and seeing angels all the time. I'm not talking about in dreams or visions or trances, I'm talking about opened-eyed visions when I would just see angels all over the place all the time. Then the ability to see God's angels just dried up! When I came back to America I was disappointed. I said, "Lord, I want to see Your angels again." God still opens my eyes and I still see His angels from time to time. But now I know that when the Lord allows me to see His angels there is a purpose for it. That purpose is to co-labor with God's angels to re-create Christ in my sphere of influence. Today, most of the time, I discern God's angels without actually having an open-eyed vision of them, and those types of angelic encounters are still just as relevant. I have learned to work with the Holy Spirit to discern the heart of heaven in reference to why the Lord has released His angels into my life. I wrote about this in great detail in the second book of this series, *Visitations of Angels and Other Supernatural Experiences II.*

When I pray for impartation, some have that gift (seer operation) activated in their life; they begin to see God's angels, they begin to see Jesus. Why? Because God is love and we need to see and discern His Son (John 14:7). I am a witness. On November 25, 2001, Jesus appeared to me. He touched my left hand and spoke to me out of Scripture, Matthew 28:18-20, and called me to go into the entire world and preach the Gospel. I am a witness that He is not dead; He is alive. I am a witness to that, and I will always share that amazing truth as long as I tarry on this side of eternity. Many times in our meetings when I share these testimonies, guess what happens? People have encounters with Jesus; they are commissioned by Jesus; they entertain the heavenly realms. Why? The testimony of Jesus is the spirit of prophecy (Revelation 19:10).

So I come back from Canada where I had this amazing visitation of Jesus. This was not a vision; the Lord appeared to me and I felt His hand touch me. This was an appearing of the Lord Jesus in bodily form. (Perhaps you would like to hear that testimony? You can download that Mp3 message at no cost by searching for "From the Gutter to Glory" in our online bookstore. "From the Gutter to Glory" is also available as a mini book (www.kingofgloryministries.org/store). I had been seeing angels everywhere I look, and all of a sudden I don't see angels anymore. I am not feeling the glory of God. But I purpose in my heart, "Lord, if You're not going to come down here, I'm going to come up there." And I began to entertain the heavenly realms. I was reading my Bible one day and this word became a rhema word to me from Hebrews chapter 13, verse 2: *"Do not forget to entertain strangers, for by so doing some have unwittingly entertained angels."* I thought, "Aha! If people can "unwittingly" entertain angels, I can entertain angels on purpose!" So I began to do so. In fact, Kathy and I still entertain angels today. We welcome them into our house. I welcome them into our meetings. I entertain them on purpose.

Teachable moment: If you want God's angels to work on your behalf, invite them to work. Recognize them and release them: "Father, I welcome and I release Your angels of miracles and supernatural provision in the name of Jesus." What happens? Creative miracles transpire in your life consistently. I am not making this stuff up. It is a real dynamic in God's Kingdom. This is one way of entertaining heaven.

Cheesy

So I told God, "I want to entertain Your angels. If people can do it without being aware of it, I'm going to do it on purpose." So I had this little house in a crack neighborhood. I didn't have any money. I had a herniated disc in my back, deafness in my ears, and a blood disease. I'd been born again, but I was being beaten up in the church. So I said, "Lord, Your Word says I can entertain your angels without being aware of it. I'm going to do it on purpose." I didn't know what I was doing. I began to pray, "Lord, I welcome Your angels, in Jesus' name. I've got ramen noodles and Kool-Aid in the refrigerator. I've got some peanut butter and crackers. And there are some cheese slices there

Heavenly Revelation and Earthly Manifestation

too." I told the angels, "You guys are all welcome to all of that stuff." Quite frankly I was not sure it was going to work, and it seemed a little cheesy at the time (pun intended).

I don't think ramen noodles and Kool-Aid were very appetizing to the angels, but I was giving all my money away so that's all I had to eat, which is another reason why I fasted a lot. You know that the Bible teaches us that angels have their own food (Psalm 78:23-25). I would just entertain the angels. I prayed, "Lord, Your angels are welcome here." Do you know what began to happen? I began to have manifestations of the Kingdom. I would go out and work and come back to that little house. I would go into my prayer room and I would begin to hear things in the kitchen. I would get up and I would run in there. I knew someone was in the little kitchen. I'd begin to smell the fragrance of heaven. That's entertaining heaven. Sometimes if I just start talking about it, it comes; the fragrance begins to manifest.

So I began to entertain heaven on purpose. This went on for months. I was hearing things happening in the house. So one night I was in my little prayer closet and I hear this ruckus outside; I hear all this commotion. I thought, "There are angels out there!" So I jump up. The last time I had done this I went out really boisterous, really noisy as I burst through the door. I thought, "This time I'm going to do it really quietly." So I got up really quietly and I tiptoed out of the prayer room and walked into the living room. There were eight angels goofing around in my living room. This was an open eyed vision. There was one big one—one I had seen in heaven with Jesus—and seven adolescent angels. They were playing and wrestling.

Oh my gosh! There are seven angels! I'm looking at them playing and running around and wrestling and making all kinds of noise. All of a sudden they stopped and turned and looked at me. They realized I could see them. I'm looking at them, they are looking at me; and I'm looking at them, they are looking at me. The big angel had his wings outspread; he was playing with the younger looking angels. He's looking at me and then he smiled at me (he had blond hair and blue eyes. I had seen him before in heaven and he comes to our meetings sometimes). So, I smiled back at him. Then all of a sudden they all started laughing and I started laughing. I said, "You know what, guys? You are welcome here." Then I went back into the prayer room praising God for answering my prayers.

From that day forward, angels were always in the house. In fact, the glory of God was always in the house. There would be times when I would come home from working and as I opened up the front door and stepped through, the power of God would hit me and I would just fall out in the Spirit. I would be slain in the Spirit. I would be unconscious on the floor. I wouldn't even close the door. I would wake up seven or eight hours later and I had been in heaven all day with Jesus.

One of my friends came over one day. We were going to go to a Christian concert. When he walked into the house, that same big angel was sitting on the couch. I could see him. My friend went over and sat down on the angel. When he did, the power of God hit him and he hit the floor. He was out; I couldn't get him up. I couldn't get him to come back to consciousness; he was out on the floor for fifteen minutes or so. We were going to be late for the concert. It was problematic. It was Amy Grant.

Heavenly Revelation and Earthly Manifestation

Finally he came to and said, "Wow, dude! What was that?"

"Well, you sat down on the angel."

It's a practical example of entertaining heaven. These things are real! It's not about me. Yes, I had an encounter and I saw Jesus; but it's not about me. God wants to do this with you. God is no respecter of persons (Romans 2:11, KJV; Acts 10:34, KJV). What God did in my life, He can do in your life.

The testimony of Jesus is the spirit of prophecy (Revelation 19:10). I want to encourage you to press in. By reading the testimonies that are in this book, there can be an activation and impartation that you can receive. I will include a prayer for activation and impartation. Pray this prayer and believe to receive activation and impartation of the seer operation.

Put your hand on your chest and pray out loud:

Lord, I ask You to reveal to me the secrets and hidden mysteries that eye has not seen and ear has not heard. Lord, I ask in Jesus' name that You ignite my heart by the power of Your Spirit. Lord, let the Kingdom of Heaven enter into my heart. Father, I'm asking You to reveal to me the mysteries and the secret things that You have prepared for those who love You. And, Lord, I love You. I ask You, Father, in the name of Jesus, to reveal the fellowship of the mysteries of the unsearchable riches found in Jesus Christ. Lord, I ask that You reveal them to me. Reveal them to my spirit. Lord, I ask that You open up to me the manifold wisdom of God. Lord, I'm asking that You would give me eyes to see and ears to hear. Lord, I'm asking that You would release to me spiritual

> *discernment to see and to hear in a new and supernatural way. Holy Spirit, I welcome You to try me. Father God, I ask You to create within me a clean heart and renew a steadfast spirit within me. In Jesus' name I pray, amen.*

I want you to stay in a posture of reception and receive as I pray over you.

> *Father, I want to thank You because of the heavens that are opening over the person reading this right now. I thank You, God, for releasing Your angels of activation and impartation that are to touch the heirs of salvation. Father, I ask You in the name of Jesus that the Spirit of wisdom and revelation would rest upon every person who is reading this.*

I sense that many of you are going to have supernatural experiences. Many of you will be taken out into the realms of heaven, even as you lie down upon your bed. Many of you will have dreams and trances and visions. I sense that some of you will have angelic visitations. Some of you will have visitations of the Lord Himself. Some of you will have revelation come to you. In fact, the Spirit of wisdom and revelation will visit many of you. Someone will be awakened at 5:04 a.m. and God will speak to you from Isaiah 50:4. God will give unto you the tongue of the learned to speak a word in due season to those who are weary. I decree over you that ministries are being birthed, and that lives are being transformed right now, in Jesus' mighty name.

> *I thank You, mighty God, that You are going to open up our eyes and ears to see and hear, in Jesus' mighty name.*

For some of you there is going to be a re-creation happening in your spiritual heart, that the eyes of your understanding that we see Ephesians 1:18 will be enlightened. It will be like a flash of light, then all of a sudden the seer operation is just going to turn on and you will begin to see and to hear in a new and supernatural way with understanding of heavenly truth. You will be sealed with supernatural discernment.

> *Thank You, Lord. Father, we welcome Your angels of activation and impartation to come and to minister to those who are heirs of salvation. Holy Spirit, we invite You to come and to touch the heirs of salvation, in Jesus' mighty name. Amen.*

CHAPTER 8

God's Angels and the Invisible Realms of the Heavenly Places

I want to tell you a bit more about the heavenly realms, particularly about the invisible realms of heaven. We will look at a few familiar passages of Scripture, beginning in the Book of Hebrews, chapter 1, starting in verses 1 and 2:

> *God, who at various times and in various ways spoke in time past to the fathers by the prophets, has in these last days spoken to us by His Son, whom He has appointed heir of all things, through whom also He made the worlds.*

Many Bible scholars believe that the Book of Hebrews was written specifically to Jewish believers. Let's study this passage going on to verse 3:

> [God's Son] *who being the brightness of His glory and the express image of His person, and upholding all things by the word of His power, when He had by Himself purged our sins, sat down at the right hand of the Majesty on high.*

When this passage of Scripture refers to "the brightness," it is translated from a Greek word that would indicate what we know today as a photo flash, though they didn't have a photo flash back then. What it means is effervescence or a flash of brightness. It is talking about Jesus being glorified, like Matthew 17:1-8 where Jesus is transfigured. Jesus is still transfigured; He can continue to be transfigured even today.

I believe that we live in a day and time when God's people can be transfigured. What that means is that as we submit fully to God, His glory, His presence, His character comes upon us. We are translated, transformed into the very image of Jesus, which enables us to re-create Christ in our sphere of influence. And part of that comes from the ability to have revelation from the unseen worlds—paradise or heaven, according to Hebrews 1:2.

This passage of Scripture in verse 3 talks about God upholding all things with His word. *Word* also refers to the Lord Jesus, but it is also talking about Creation in context. This is again a Hebraism. We looked at Genesis 1:1 previously how God created the heavens, the heavenly realms (remember this is plural), but He also created the terrestrial realm or the earth. And all of these things are upheld by His Word, which is His Son Jesus. It should be noted that some theologians believe that the terrestrial or earthly realm is a part of the second heaven. Revelation 12:9 hints at this possibility: *"So the great dragon was cast out, that serpent of old, called the devil and satan, who deceives the whole world; he was cast to the earth, and his angels were cast out with him."* I can verify that I have seen a lot of demons upon the earth! Of course, greater is He who is in you than he who is in the world (1 John 4:4)!

Created by Him

God created all things, as it says in Colossians 1, all things were created by Him and for His purposes (v. 16). Some of these things are invisible to us. That does not invalidate the reality of them, nor does it invalidate our ability to discern them, to step into them, to entertain them, or to operate in them. I am referring to things that are holy and of God. These are elements and attributes of the Godly dimensions. Many times as we entertain heaven these elements take the form of revelation or the spirit of wisdom and revelation.

What Hebrews 1:1-3 is describing is your role as a royal priest according to the order of Melchizedek. Let's go on with verses 4 and 5:

> [God's Son] *having become so much better than the angels, as He has by inheritance obtained a more excellent name than they. For to which of the angels did He ever say: "You are My Son, Today I have begotten You"?*

Continuing with Hebrews 1:5-6:

> *And again: "I will be to Him a Father, And He shall be to Me a Son"? But when He again brings the firstborn into the world, He says: "Let all the angels of God worship Him."*

The word here translated "world" is different than what we think of in our Western mindsets. It means the habitable or visible realm. So, you see, God created a habitable or visible realm that we call the terrestrial realm or the earth; but God also created invisible realms. That's what I want to press in on here so that you can have a biblical understanding of the invisible realms that God created, because by Him all things were created both visible and invisible. Just because we cannot see them, that does not invalidate their existence or their importance.

Now verse 7:

> And of the angels He says: "Who makes His angels spirits
> And His ministers a flame of fire."

I teach in depth on that at our school Angels, Miracles, Signs, and Wonders because there is a correlation between God's angels and miracles signs and wonders. The word in this verse translated "spirits" is *pneumata* in the Greek. What it means is an angel, a demon, or a spirit. This passage is obviously referring to God's angels. There is a difference between angels and God's angels. Remember that there are fallen angels which are rightly called demons.

Going on with verse 8:

> But to the Son He says: "Your throne, O God, is forever and ever; A scepter of righteousness is the scepter of Your kingdom."

The Mantle of Melchizedek

Now this passage speaks of the rod of royal authority. It speaks of a diadem given by Elohim. I want to prophesy to you that you are called to be a royal priest according to the order of Melchizedek. And as we grow and allow the Spirit of God transform who we are, I believe that Elohim, the Father of Jesus, is releasing His power to His friends at this hour.

This is a different level of heavenly power. This type of heavenly power is different than the anointing of the Holy Spirit. I am not saying it is greater, only different. It is the scepter of God the Father. It is the power of the Father (John 14:10). And when God releases to you the scepter of power, you will be able to speak to things like mountains and they will be removed. You will be able to speak to things like tornadoes and hurricanes and they will cease. You will be able to work incredible signs and wonders in the name of Jesus Christ. As you discern revelation and get authorization from heaven (the Father), you will be empowered to decree or to speak needful things into existence. On the other hand you may be given the power to speak to hurricanes and other types of storms and command them to cease! This is all an obtainable part and aspect of the Kingdom of God for you today. We do not always have to see these kinds of heavenly power or anointing, just discern them to operate in them.

The Kingdom of Jesus is a heavenly place. It is not visible to most of us at this point in this lifetime on the terrestrial realm because we have not exercised our spiritual senses by reason of use to discern the invisible attributes of God's Kingdom; but we can. (See Hebrews 5:14.) Really what I am referring to is learning to operate in the mantle or the anointing of Melchizedek in this lifetime. We have access to the heavenly places and can go behind the veil to receive revelation of the Father's destinies for our lives and call those destinies into existence on the earthly realm with our words.

Again, speaking of the Lord Jesus, Hebrews 1, verse 9 and the beginning of verse 10 say:

> "You have loved righteousness and hated lawlessness; Therefore God, Your God, has anointed You With the oil of gladness more than Your companions." And: "You, LORD, in the beginning laid the foundation of the earth."

This is another Hebraism that goes back to the testimony of the creation of the worlds. Going on with verse 10, we read,

> And: "You LORD, in the beginning laid the foundation of the earth, And the heavens are the work of Your hands."

The Mindset of Heaven

In this passage of Scripture, the Greek word translated "heavens" is *ouranos*, which means the heavenly abode or the area above the sky that we can see. This is referring to Psalm 102:25. It is important that we understand that the Hebrew mindset of heaven and the Greek mindset of heaven are two different things. What I am trying to do here is encourage you to cultivate a Hebraic mindset of the Kingdom of Heaven. Let's have a look at Psalm 102, verse 25, for the sake of this teaching.

> *Of old You laid the foundation of the earth* [terrestrial realm], *And the heavens* [plural] *are the work of Your hands.*

In this passage the word translated "heavens" is the Hebrew word *shamayim*, that we said before can mean the celestial world or the dwelling place of God and other heavenly beings. When the New Testament was written, they did not have a Greek word that fit exactly or translated correctly for the

Hebraic understanding of heaven. What I want you to see is that there is a Hebraic understanding of heaven or heavenly realms that is different from our Greek or Western mindset of heaven.

What I am trying to tell you is that "heaven" is not always up but it is also all around us. We don't always have to die to go to heaven. The Bible says to be absent from the body is to be present with the Lord (2 Corinthians 5:8), and we've often taken that to mean in our Western church society that when we die we go to heaven. And that is very true; but it is only part of the truth. The truth is that we can be absent from the body and present with the Lord in this lifetime. We can entertain the heavenly realms. This can be in the form of visionary experiences or it can also be in the form of a supernatural knowledge which is called the unction or anointing of the Holy Spirit (1 John 2:20).

Let me finalize the scripture in Hebrews 1. Let's look at verses 10-12:

> And: "You, LORD, in the beginning laid the foundation of the earth, And the heavens are the work of Your hands. They will perish, but You remain; And they will all grow old like a garment; Like a cloak You will fold them up...

God is saying He will fold up the earth. Think about that. Continuing with verse 12 and 13 the scriptures say:

> ...And they will be changed. But You are the same, And Your years will not fail." But to which of the angels has He

ever said: "Sit at My right hand, Till I make Your enemies Your footstool"?

This is speaking about Melchizedek again. I believe that God is raising up in this lifetime a royal priesthood according to the order of Melchizedek that will rule and reign with the scepter (the rod of the Father) in their hand, and they will be able to release the Kingdom of God with great power. For those who would like to release the Kingdom of God with great power, sometimes it comes from being able to understand the attributes of the heavenly realms that we have not yet seen.

You are called to live in this kind of power and anointing today.

You are called to discern or see heavenly truth and to release those heavenly revelations upon the earth. You are called to live a life of power and delegated authority (Luke 9:1-2). Let's just keep it simple and do the works of Jesus; preach the Kingdom of God and to heal the sick. You can learn to work miracles, signs, and wonders. In the next chapter we will look at several supernatural keys that can enable and empower you to step into your Christ-centered destiny.

CHAPTER 9

God Created the Invisible Realms of Heaven

Hebrews, chapter 11, gives us some further insight into the invisible realms of heaven. I believe that many of you reading this book are going to discern the invisible. As you pray the activation prayer in this book, I believe many of you who have never had a vision, never encountered heaven, never seen an angel, never experienced the heavenly realms can be released into that realm immediately as you read the message and as you press in to the invisible realms or entertain heaven.

When I talk about the invisible realm, I'm talking about the same invisible realm that we just read about in Hebrews, chapter 1; the same realm that God created in the beginning in Genesis 1—the heavens and the earth, the invisible domain of God. Let's talk about that. Hebrews 11:1: *"Now faith is the substance of things hoped for, the evidence of things not seen."*

This is talking about the invisible realm. In the invisible realms in the Kingdom of God, faith is a tangible substance. Jesus said to the woman with the issue of blood, *"Your faith has made you well"* (Mark 5:34). Several times in Scripture Jesus said things like, "Your faith has made you whole," or, "According to your faith let it be done unto you." You see, your faith is the currency of Christ. Your faith in the invisible realm of the Kingdom is a tangible substance. It is visible; it's heavenly. Your faith is a tangible substance of great value in the heavenly places. Both the Lord and His angels can see and discern your faith in the heavenly dimensions.

By Faith the Worlds Were Framed

Now to Hebrews 11:2-3: *"For by it the elders obtained a good testimony. By faith we understand that the worlds were framed..."* Again, the author of Hebrews was speaking in a Hebraism. It is speaking about the story of Creation from the Torah in Genesis 1. Going on with Hebrews 11:3: *"...the worlds were framed by the word of God..."* We just saw that in Hebrews, chapter 1. Chapter 11, verse 3, continues: *"...so that the things which are seen were not made of things which are visible."*

So what the author of Hebrews is saying is when God created the heavens (plural) and the earth, they were made of intangible elements. They were made of things which cannot be visibly seen, or things that are invisible to you and me as we inhabit the earthly or terrestrial realm. So in other words, the book in your hands, the shoes on your feet, the chair you are sitting in, are all made of invisible things that have been manifested in the earthly realm by the word of God.

Jesus our Role Model

We are created in God's image. Remember we learned in Genesis 1:26 that God said, *"Let Us make man in Our image,"* and God also made the heavens and the terrestrial realm, the heavens (plural) and the earth. God made you and me in His image to have dominion over both realms—the heavenly realms and the earthly realm. If we are created in God's image and learn to yield the scepter of power in our hands, we can minister the way God the Father ministers; we can minister the way Jesus ministers. I am not saying we are God; I'm not talking about new Dominion Theology. I am talking about what the Scripture says: we are created in God's image. Jesus is fully God but He was fully man. He came to earth in the form of a man born of a virgin. But as He grew, as He matured, as He learned about the Kingdom of Heaven on earth as a human being, He was transformed (Matthew 17:2 and Mark 9:2), He was filled with the Holy Spirit (Luke 3:22; 4:1), and Jesus grew in knowledge and stature with both God and man (Luke 2:52). He grew in the knowledge of God's Kingdom. You can too.

The Lord Jesus grew in His knowledge of the power or ability to yield His scepter of authority, which we have been learning about in Hebrews 1. You can study it also in Psalm 110. That is why Jesus could say, *"If you say to this mountain, 'Be removed and cast into the sea,' it will be done"* (Matthew 21:21). That's why Jesus could say to the fig tree, "Die!" and it would die (v. 19). That's why He could speak to the storm and it would cease (Mark 4:39; Matthew 8:26). That's why Jesus could speak to leprosy and it would dissolve (Matthew 8:3). That is why He could speak to demons and they would come out with a single word (Matthew 17:18). All of this was because He recognized He could employee or make use of the scepter and authority of God His Father as He ministered upon the earth (John 14:10).

Yield the Scepter of Power

And at this hour God is raising up a royal priesthood of His friends (both men and women—royal kings and queens) who will yield and learn to employee the scepter of God's power, who have the authority to speak and create because we are created in His image. Some of you reading this have seen it function as a word of knowledge is called out, such as God doing dental miracles and gold crowns appearing in someone's mouth. God can do many other things. We have not scratched the surface as to what is available to us and what amazing things God has given us the power and authority to do (like multiply bread or hundred dollar bills, for example). As we see evil things in the world causing harm to God's people, I would encourage you to speak death to these things just like Jesus commanded the fig tree to die.

Let's look at Hebrews 11:1 again: *"Now faith is the substance of things hoped for, the evidence of things not seen."* This is speaking of the heavenly or invisible realms. Now read verse 3: *"By faith we understand that the worlds were framed by the word of God, so that the things which are seen were not made of things which are visible."*

Seek the Kingdom First

In other words, there are invisible things in God's Kingdom that we can decree which will manifest in the natural realm. Does that make sense? We need to understand that the Kingdom of God is an invisible place to us who inhabit the terrestrial realm, but it is real even though the Kingdom of Heaven is invisible. It's tangible in both the spiritual realms and the earthly dimensions. This is a supernatural conundrum, much like the Kingdom itself. We can step into it as we learn to entertain it. We need to have our mindsets transformed. We need to have our minds renewed; we need to have our minds transformed so that we can focus on heavenly things, not on earthly things.

One of my favorite passages of Scripture in this season is Isaiah 26:3: *"You will keep him in perfect peace, Whose mind is stayed on You."* The concept is we keep our mind focused on Jesus like a laser beam. When we hear, "Well, the economy is bad"; we need to learn to immediately think, "I shall prosper and be in health" (3 John 1:2). I call this kind of heavenly mindedness—thought prayers; and thought prayers are a supernatural key to become triumphant in your prayer life every day!

One day a friend whose car was broken down called me for help. He needed a tow. I told him to lay hands on his car and to pray for it (I saw this in a short vision). But he asked again, "Can you give me a tow?" Again I told him to lay hands on it and pray for his car **now**. So he prayed for it, and instantly his engine started running. It started working! This really worked to increase my friend's faith too.

You see, we are not of this realm. We need a different mindset.

Riches in Glory

Once I felt like I had symptoms of a cold coming on. So I asked Kathy to lay hands on me and pray for my healing in the name of Jesus. I don't need any cold medication. I asked for prayer for my healing from the spirit of cold. I received my healing by faith when Kathy laid her hands upon me and prayed for me rebuking the spirit of cold! Try it sometime!

We want to think about the Kingdom first.

Once my tax bill was due, so I prayed. *"Father, I thank You right now in Jesus' name that you will supply all of my needs according to Your riches in glory."* The Holy Spirit said, "Go and check your check box." (We call our post office box our check box because we expect to get checks and not bills all of the time.) So I go to the post office. Behold! There's a check in there that covers the tax bill. This is Kingdom finance! We entertain heaven and receive guidance, and then we just do what the Lord shows us to do.

How does that happen? We decree things in the unseen realm and they manifest in the natural realm. If we can press in to this aspect of God's Kingdom, we can water our minds with this type of Scripture and we can focus on the Kingdom of God through worship, through prayer, by listening over and over to teachings on this subject that are from the word of God. I do that. Why? I want the revelations of the Kingdom of Heaven to get into my spirit. I want the revelations of the Kingdom of Heaven to become tangible. I want the revelations of the Kingdom of Heaven to activate my faith and supernaturally resonate within my spirit man. I have a faith in me; I'm a lot bigger on the inside than I am on the outside. I want my faith to be activated, to grow into mature faith. You should desire for your faith to grow into mature faith too.

The Law of Observation

Whatever you look at, whatever you listen to is what you will become. If you look at all the crises in the world, you are going to be overcome by fear. If you look at the financial crises that are happening; you are going to be overcome by fear. If you look at the international leaders who clamor about war and you focus on that, you are also going to become overcome with trepidation and fear. But if you look at the Kingdom of God and you take your place in the heavenly realms, from heaven you can decree peace and decree that political issues like this will be supernaturally resolved. Don't focus on wars and rumors of wars and scud missiles. Focus on the fact that political issues like this will be supernaturally resolved in Jesus' mighty name. Get God's heart on the matter and speak this into existence.

Let's go to Colossians, chapter 1, verses 3-5:

> *We give thanks to the God and Father of our Lord Jesus Christ, praying always for you, since we heard of your faith in Christ Jesus and of your love for all the saints; because of the hope which is laid up for you in heaven...*

You see, there is a hope; there is a calling laid up for you in heavenly places. Now let's skip to verse 9:

> *For this reason we also, since the day we heard it, do not cease to pray for you, and to ask that you may be filled with the knowledge of His will in all wisdom and spiritual understanding.*

What does that mean? That means revelation of the unseen realm. Now verse 10:

> *That you may walk worthy of the Lord, fully pleasing Him, being fruitful in every good work and increasing in the knowledge of God.*

What does it mean to walk fully pleasing to Him? It means to have spiritual understanding and increase in the revelatory knowledge of God and in your understanding the invisible realms of heaven. It is pleasing to the Lord for you to discern correctly. Going on with verses 11-12:

> [May you be] *strengthened with all might, according to His glorious power, for all patience and longsuffering with joy; giving thanks to the Father who has qualified us to be partakers of the inheritance of the saints in the light.*

Did you know you had an inheritance as a saint of light? Your inheritance as a saint of light is not on the terrestrial realm. Your inheritance is in the spiritual realm; your inheritance is in the heavenly places; your inheritance is in the invisible realms. Now the question becomes, how do I move my inheritance as a saint of light from the invisible realms into the terrestrial realm or the visible realm. It's very simple: you begin to access the invisible realm. You learn to discern and entertain the heavenly places.

You begin to discern it according to Hebrews 5:14: *"Those who are of full age, that is, those who by reason of use have their senses exercised to discern both good and evil."* This passage teaches us about discerning the difference in spiritual dynamics and increasing in our personal spiritual discernment (1 Corinthians 12:10).

There is a place where we can activate our ability to understand spiritual things, to understand attributes of the invisible realms. It is our inheritance according to Colossians 1:12 because, through the finished work of Jesus Christ, we have been qualified to become partakers of the inheritance of the saints of light. Colossians 1, verses 13 and 14:

> [God] *has delivered us from the power of darkness and conveyed* [translated] *us into the kingdom of the Son of His love, in whom we have redemption through His blood, the forgiveness of sins.*

This is an important point. In Colossians 1:15-16, speaking of the Messiah, Jesus, we read:

> *He is the image of the invisible God, the firstborn over all creation. For by Him all things were created that are in heaven and that are on earth, visible and invisible, whether thrones or dominions or principalities or powers. All things were created through Him and for Him.*

In the beginning at the creation of the earth, God created the heavens and He created all the spiritual beings that inhabit the invisible places (God's angels and even demons or fallen angels). They were all created for God's purposes. They are still utilized for His purposes. These created spiritual beings inhabit an invisible realm or invisible spiritual dimensions. I love Moravian Falls, North Carolina, it is a beautiful place. We have many spiritual gates here; portals, if you will, into heavenly places. However, it should be noted (as I stated previously) that not all the gates or portals (open heavens) here in Moravian Falls lead to the Godly dimensions.

The issue becomes our lack of discernment to tell the difference between the holy and the profane or unholy (Ezekiel 44:23), the good and the evil. So people come to Moravian Falls, North Carolina, seeking spiritual experiences and they tap into the invisible realm. The problem is that sometimes they tap into the demonic realms and they don't know the difference. You need to know the difference. You need to exercise your spiritual senses by reason of use so you can learn to discern between good and evil; so that you can discern the difference between what is really heavenly and what appears to be heavenly.

It's important that we understand this; because if we seek to access the invisible realms of heaven, we need to be mature. We need to be walking in right relationship with God. We need to be walking in holiness and sanctification. This is not something you want to do willy-nilly; it's something you need to do soberly. In the next chapter we will look at several ways that you can rightly entertain the heavenly places to receive supernatural direction and learn to walk in God's perfect will for your life.

CHAPTER 10

The Hidden and Mysterious Treasures of the Kingdom of Heaven

In Colossians, chapter 2, Paul speaks about the church of Laodicea; he talks about how many had not actually seen him. Then in verses 2 and 3 Paul tells the impact of that:

> *that their hearts may be encouraged, being knit together in love, and attaining to all riches of the full assurance of understanding, to the knowledge of the mystery of God, both of the Father and of Christ, in whom are hidden all the treasures of wisdom and knowledge.*

Paul is speaking about the hidden mysteries of the Kingdom of Heaven in the invisible realms. I believe that the Apostle Paul had revelations that he was not able to share fully because God would not release him to do so. He hints about it. I believe Paul had a great understanding of the hidden, mysterious things in God's Kingdom; the invisible realms of God's Kingdom; open heavens. Let's touch on it quickly and go to 2 Corinthians 12. Paul is speaking of himself accessing the invisible realm. This passage speaks of entertaining heaven. He relays it in great humility. Verse 1 begins, *"It is doubtless not profitable for me to boast. I will come to visions and revelations of the Lord."*

Would you like to be able to say that? It's OK. God wants you to come to visions and revelations of Him. Remember what we learned previously in Colossians 1; it gives God pleasure when we walk in the fullness of wisdom and revelation. God wants us to come into visions and revelations of the Lord. These visions and revelations are not going to happen for the most part in the terrestrial realm; they are going to happen in the invisible realms where we learn to entertain heaven. But we must access the heavenly realms with maturity and with great discernment nonetheless.

One Minute in Heaven

The word translated "visions" means supernatural visions, trances, or seeing into the unseen realm or seeing into heavenly places. The word translated "revelations" means uncovered mysteries or uncovered heavenly secrets. Do you want some of that? I believe you can have it.

Let me tell you: one minute in the real realm of heaven, one minute in the tangible, real glory of God can transform your life. One minute in the heavenly places, one word from Jesus in such an experience can transform who you are in Christ more than hours of teaching from a pulpit. One moment in the heavenly realms where you have an encounter with the King of kings and Lord of lords, where you experience the tangible presence of the glory of God can transform your life instantly. One legitimate word from the King can release you into greater revelation and wisdom about the realms of His Kingdom.

As much as I enjoy preaching or hearing anointed preaching, I want to be in the glory. I want to come to visions and revelations. Being in the glory of God is what enabled me to write books. I will come to visions and revelations. All the books I have written came from visions and revelations. Two hours in the glory, 80,000 words. Are you a pastor? Do you have a difficult time sometimes coming up with a sermon for Sunday morning? One minute in the glory of God can give you a whole month's worth of sermons.

So we can glean heavenly revelation from the invisible realm or heavenly places. I love this passage of Scripture in 2 Corinthians 12:1: *"It is doubtless not profitable for me to boast. I will come to visions and revelations of the Lord."*

Put your hand on your chest and say it out loud: *"I will come to visions and revelations of the Lord, in Jesus' name, amen."*

The spirit of religion wants to tell you that kind of mindset is proud and haughty. That is a lie straight from the pit of hell because God desires for you to come to visions and revelations of Him. The enemy wants to deceive you; he wants to steal your inheritance as a saint of light. The enemy does not want you to come to visions and revelations of God. The enemy wants to keep you in the bondage of religion and in ignorance of the reality of the Kingdom of Heaven in the now; he wants to keep you rooted and grounded in the terrestrial realm. The accuser wants to keep you grounded in sin; he wants to keep you tethered to the carnal realm and works overtime to make your ears heavy and your eyes dull (Isaiah 6:10).

But Jesus wants to cut that tether through the power of the finished work of the Cross, through the blood of the Messiah, and with the Sword of the Spirit. The Lord desires for you to rise up into the heavenly places to be seated with Christ, to come into visions and revelations, to see and hear hidden mysteries and revelations from the Kingdom of God. Of course all such visions and heavenly revelation must line up with Scripture, and you must be submitted to authority. But God wants you to have supernatural encounters.

Paul, going on in 2 Corinthians 12:2, doesn't say it is him; but we know it is.

> *I know a man in Christ who fourteen years ago—whether in the body I do not know, or whether out of the body I do not know, God knows—such a one was caught up to the third heaven.*

The word translated "heaven" is the Greek *ouranou*, meaning heavenly places. He was caught up into heaven. In verse 4 we read: *"He was caught up into Paradise and heard inexpressible words, which it is not lawful for a man to utter."*

The word translated "Paradise" means heaven or a garden or an "Eden," possibly a place of future happiness. We look at heaven as something that is going to happen in the future. Heaven is happening now. There is a lot of activity in heaven right now. Right now around the throne of God there is business taking place. Right now Jesus is seated on the throne at the right hand of the Father and He is praying for you; He's praying for me. Heaven is already unfolding in your life right now. You just need to learn to discern it and then walk in heavenly perfect plans for your life every day.

In fact, the Scripture tells us Jesus already prayed for the message of this book before I was ever born because in heaven time as we know it does not exist. That is why I am not bound by time. I am not a slave to time. I take authority over time as part of my inheritance as a saint of light. How do I get so much stuff done? I take authority over time. How have I written fourteen books so quickly? I took authority over time. I get into my office and quote what I learned from Joshua Mills:

> *Father, I thank You that time is my servant. I am not time's servant. And I thank You, Lord, that You are going to give me favor with time. I release angels of the Most High God, angels of creative miracles and supernatural provision to go into my calendar and the calendar of my days. I thank You, Lord, that I am going to get more done today than I got done all last week. I thank You this is going to be the most fruitful year of the ministry, in Jesus' name.*

Guess what's happening? It is the most fruitful year of the ministry in Jesus' mighty name. So you can do the same thing because time is an invisible thing. You can take authority over the invisible. You can call those things that are not as though they are, according to Romans 4:17. Time as we know it does not exist in heaven.

Remember we looked at Colossians 1 where God created everything for His purposes (v. 16). We looked at the story of Creation in Genesis 1. God created the sun and the moon for times and seasons (v. 14). God created time for His purposes. And if we are God's children created in His image, we can take authority over time.

Do you wonder if that is biblical? What about Joshua? He spoke to the sun and it stood still at the word of the Lord. I believe the return of Jesus is close at hand. So, that's all the more reason for us to take authority over time—an invisible substance. You have that privilege as a king and a priest; you have that privilege as a member of God's family. As the grace of God comes upon your life, the Lord can actually give you the anointing to take authority over time like Joshua at this hour (pun intended).

Actually, at this hour the days on earth have literally begun to grow shorter in the natural realm. That is another reason that we need to redeem the days. It is also an indication that the return of the Lord is at hand. On Friday March 11, 2011, an 8.9 magnitude earthquake struck Northeast of Japan. The result of this intense earthquake caused planet earth to shift or move upon its figure axis about six and one-half inches. This resulted in each day becoming shorter in length by about 1.8 microseconds. Scientists have also theorized that other major earthquakes have also added to the shorting of the length of earth days.[1]

All of these things we are talking about hinge on our ability to discern the invisible realm. I believe that is possible because of the open heavens. We talked about that from Luke 3:21; Jesus prayed, the heavens opened. And we have also talked about how they never closed. Sometimes they are brass over our head because of our sin, or maybe because of the sin of the people in our nation or the sin of the people in our region.

Piggy Back

But as an individual, you can press into heaven. You can break through into the heavens opening up over your head and over your life. And once you get that breakthrough, other people can piggyback on your breakthrough. Sometimes people piggyback on our breakthrough. I give God glory for that. I have many testimonies of people who have broken into the open heaven and access their inheritance of the saints of light where they see Jesus. They get into the glory. Their lives begin to transform.

It is not something you can put into words; I can't tell you how to do this in an A, B, C, D style; I can't write a manual on it. It is a faith walk. It is a Kingdom dynamic. I can only tell you to seek first the Kingdom of God and His righteousness and all these things will be added unto you (Matthew 6:33).

I believe there is a grace of God for all of us to prosper and be in health in this hour (3 John 1:2). Part of that has to do with the fact that we can access the invisible places. I want to touch on this one more time. I believe that there are places where the heavens are open and in those places there is free access into the heavenly realms or the invisible realms. I believe the place where I live (from time to time) and where we host many conferences, *near* Moravian Falls, North Carolina, has an open heaven.

I saw a 150-foot angel at one of my conferences and the Holy Spirit told me he was positioned there to guard the open heaven. The enemy doesn't want you to have an open heaven; he wants the heavens to be brass over your head; he wants you to labor and toil at religious activities each week. But God is telling His people to be diligent to enter into His rest, to enter into His presence, to enter into His glory and allow Him to work on your behalf (Hebrews 4:10-11).

When you rest in His presence, when you rest in His glory and the heavens open up over your life, it's no longer a plow. Things just happen. Hallelujah! Grace and favor chase you down. Have you seen the special programs on nature that show lions chasing down their prey? How would you like to experience God's grace and favor chasing you down and jumping on you like that? When you begin to rest in God and access these invisible realms, the realms of the Kingdom, one minute in the legitimate glory of God and you come out of that invisible realm, you come out of the heavenly realms, it's like the grace of God just chases you down. Everything you touch prospers. It's no longer problematic.

The Lord Will Open Storehouses in Heaven

I want to recap a scripture from Deuteronomy 28. This passage is all about blessings and curses. I want to encourage you to study it. But in reference to windows, doors, or heavens being open over your life; if we are obedient to God, if we are doing the first things first, if we are faithful with our tithes and offerings, if we are walking in holiness, if we are not murdering our brothers and sisters with our tongues, God promises, starting with verse 12, *"The LORD will open to you His good treasure, the heavens...."*

Powerful Heavenly Blessings

The literal translation means the storehouse of heaven. There are storehouses in heaven; storehouses that have many things: finances, body parts, grace, favor. There are millions of angels in the heavenly realms that are just waiting to be released upon the earth to minister for heirs of salvation (Hebrews 1:14). Do you know how they are released? They are released when the heavens open and God rains out a blessing. When we learn to discern this dynamic of heaven we can step into God blessings each and every day of our lives.

> *The LORD will open to you His good treasure, the heavens, to give the rain to your land in its season, and to bless all the work of your hand. You shall lend to many nations, but you shall not borrow.*

God opens up the heavens and it begins to rain down blessings upon you. God blesses the works of your hands. The key is that you have to set your hand to something ordained by God. There are certain blessings you cannot get in the earthly realm. There is a way that you can get impartation, such as Romans 1:11, where a man can lay hands on you and give you a terrestrial or earthly impartation; it's carnal. It's good, but it is not on the same level as a heavenly impartation directly from the Lord. When the heavens open up, God can pour out blessings upon you; God can pour out anointings upon you. Those heavenly blessings are special. They are powerful. These are the Father's blessings designed especially for you and your needs.

I believe you have positioned yourself to receive activation and impartation because of the day and hour in which we live. The heavens are opening; God is getting ready to pour out blessings. Romans, chapter 4, outlines this in verse 17, speaking of Abraham, the father of many nations, Paul says, *"God, who gives life to the dead and calls those things which do not exist as though they did."*

I discerned as I preparing this book that there is going to be a supernatural activation, there is going to be an open heaven released into your life as you read this book. And in that place you are going to be able to communicate directly with God. You are going to be able to call those things that do not exist as though they did. I believe the heavens are opening where you are right now, even as you are reading this. The angels of the Lord are ready to descend into your presence and to minister for those who are heirs of salvation, as we saw earlier in Hebrews 1:14.

I would encourage you to put some soaking music on and find a comfortable place. You can kneel or lie down and seek the Lord. I am going to believe God to open up the heavens for you right now. I believe many of you are going to have an experience; many are going to have your eyes open to see. I encourage you to press into this for a while. Then we will see what God does in your life to bless you and the works of your hands.

As you are becoming comfortable, I will give you some instruction. You may smell the fragrance of heaven as ozone or roses or spices. It can be very subtle. You may just have a thought or maybe you see a fleeting image; just lean into that and ask the Holy Spirit to help you. Maybe you will see a cloud; maybe you will see a tricycle. Then just ask the Holy Spirit: "Why am I seeing that cloud? Why am I seeing that tricycle?" It may continue to unfold. If you find yourself in the heavenly places, the first thing you want to do is to look at your hands and your feet. What type of clothes are you wearing? What are you standing on? As you begin to see your feet or your hands, look out further and further; then ask the Holy Spirit to show you what it is you are supposed to see.

This activation will be supernaturally released by the grace of God and though the power of the Holy Spirit because the heavens are opening over you right now! I believe the anointing of the Lord, the glory of the Lord can be upon you wherever you are reading this right now. I am going to pray over you and we will seek the Lord. We are going to ask God the Father to give us our inheritance as children and the saints of light.

I sense that for some of you reading this that God is going to give you wisdom and revelation and understanding and you are going to have a pattern revealed to you of what your assigned and ordained good work is going to be: how you are to do it, when you are to do it, where you are to do it, and with whom you are to do it.

One of the things you may experience is the Lord may begin to speak to you about a circumstance. You can begin to decree from the heavenly places what the Lord shows you. There will be a swift synchronization between what God speaks to you in the heavenly realms and what unfold on the terrestrial realm; in other words, an almost instantaneous answer to your prayers.

You are going to begin to entertain heaven wherever you are.

Prayer of Activation

Father, I thank You for the wonderful saints reading this now. I pray right now, Lord, and I ask that You would fill us with the knowledge of Your will for each of us. Lord,

I ask that You would release to us wisdom and spiritual understanding. Father, I'm asking that You would help us to discern, to see, to taste, to smell, to touch the unseen realm. I ask, Father God, in Jesus' name, that You would give us spiritual understanding. I cover each of us in the blood of Jesus. I ask You, Father God, that we would see nothing except what You would have us to see; that we would have no visions, no dreams, no trances, no supernatural encounters except those that were ordained by God the Father, God the Son, and God the Holy Spirit. And, Lord, I thank You that the heavens are open in this place, right now.

Lord, Your angels are welcome to descend even now to minister for those who are heirs of salvation. Father, we thank You that it is fully pleasing to You that each of us would be fruitful in every good work and that we would increase in the knowledge of You.

Father, I ask You today that we would be strengthened with Your might and Your glorious power. Father, I thank You that we are already qualified through the blood of Jesus Christ and the finished work of the Cross to be partakers of our heavenly inheritance as saints of light. Lord, I ask that You would convey us even now into the invisible realms of the Kingdom of Your Son, the Lord Jesus Christ of Nazareth. Help me to discern and entertain heaven right now, Lord.

Father, I just thank You that we have an inheritance of light that we can access through the finished work of Jesus Christ on the Cross. Father, we thank You that the Cross of Jesus is the bridge that opens up the heavenly places to us. And, Lord, I thank You that we are seated in the heavenly places with Christ Jesus. Lord, we give You the praise and the honor and the glory for everything You've done, everything You are doing, and everything You are going to do, in Jesus' mighty name, amen.

Please feel free to repeat this prayer of activation consistently until you get your breakthrough. Please feel free to repeat this prayer of activation out loud after you have finished reading the second part of this book as well.

Part Two

Visions of the Heavenly Places

INTRODUCTION 2

Visions of Heaven

In the next several chapters I will share several testimonies of entertaining heaven. Many of these heavenly encounters happened nearly two decades ago. I pray that you are blessed and encouraged by these experiences. Allow me to say that I am not sure about the actual dynamics of these heavenly visitations. Perhaps I was allowed by the grace of God to visit the heavenly places or heavenly realms in my spirit. In other words, these would be visions or trances. Over the years many people have questioned me about these supernatural visions, and rightly so. Some of these people have only good intentions and others people have questionable intentions. In the first part of this book I personally encouraged you to develop your personal spiritual discernment. Please use your discernment as you continue to read.

As a new believer I learned to access or entertain heaven or the heavenly places. I will depict and describe heaven and these heavenly encounters in the subsequent chapters. Soon I discovered that when I emulated the things that I saw in heavenly places upon earth there was a swift synchronization between heaven and earth in my life. In other words, my prayers were answered in a swift and supernatural way. Many times my heavenly prayers were nearly instantly answered!

I learned that by entertaining heaven I could become triumphant in prayer. This revelation transformed my life in a very short timeframe as the Lord took me from poverty to prosperity, from sickness to health, and from hopelessness to hope. I learned the reality and the power of answered prayer. In this book I have sought to outline for you the reality of entertaining heaven and it's correlation to becoming triumphant in your prayer life. I pray that you learn to become supernaturally syncopated with heaven upon the earth (John 5:19)

For example, there were many times in this season of heavenly visitations when I would weep in heaven. Yet some people teach that there will be no tears in heaven. That may be true. Perhaps my body was still upon the earth whilst my spirit had ascended into the heavenly places. Honestly, I am not sure or certain. Nor could I ever claim to be certain on this side of eternity. My only prayer is that you are edified by these testimonies and drawn closer to Jesus as Lord. The Kingdom of Heaven can at times be a conundrum.

My intention in writing these testimonies at this time (2017) is to be obedient to the Lord and to write down the visions that He instructed me to document and to scribe or write. You see, I am much more concerned with what the Lord will say to me and about me than what the people here on earth would say or write about me. One day, and *of this I am sure*, we will all stand before the judgment seat of the Lord and give an account of our works (Matthew 12:26; Hebrews 4:13; Revelation 20:12). So were these testimonies examples of being translated in the spirit? I am not sure. I can only say that the things that I experienced were life changing and have served to transform my life and draw me into a closer relationship with the Lord. May these testimonies also draw you closer to the Lord as well.

Many of the concepts and things that I saw and learned in the heavenly places all those years ago still bear life and fruit in my life today. I have seen a lot of miracles manifest upon the earth as I prayed and loosed the things I have seen in heaven (as the Holy Spirit leads and allows). Much of this has to do with learning to co-labor with God's angels to release healings and miracles upon the earth as I am led by the Holy Spirit. Allow me to say that all of these supernatural dynamics of the Kingdom of Heaven are a supernatural learning curve. Many of my friends call these kinds of supernatural manifestations of the Kingdom the "operation of the seer anointing." I once heard a very wise minister say this: "Don't judge what you do not understand," concerning the mysterious works of the Holy Spirit. That is good advice. Having said all of that we all need great discernment in these last and glorious days!

God is amazing and He is all powerful. When we begin to decide with our carnal minds what God is and is not capable of, we then put ourselves into the position of becoming like God. We can become a judge, and that is never good (Matthew 7). I would venture to say that such a mindset and place is a dangerous place to be. That kind of pride and absolute certainty in our own theology and doctrines can be the height of a religious spirit. I'm just sayin'.

As a new believer I just thought that nothing was impossible with God. It seemed that the Lord liked that mindset and He rewarded me as I was diligent to seek Him and His Kingdom. Now relax and join me as we visit the heavenly places together.

I will describe heavenly places in great detail and hopefully give the reader glimpses into the realms of heaven. Along this journey we will also see how angels move about, appear, and seem to "work" in the heavenly realms. May we all greet one another in that place one day! Heaven is real! And Christ has already prepared a place for you to dwell with Him in paradise. Your heavenly home awaits you. I pray that you too will learn to entertain heaven.

CHAPTER 11

The Father's House

I turned to see a pair of ancient doors set into the walls of the castle on the balcony. These were remarkably large and hinged in what appeared to be gold. There were also two large circular handles, one on each door. At that moment the door on the left opened. A large angel stepped out and motioned for me to enter. He had golden brown hair and was powerful, yet he had a kind and compassionate smile. It seemed that he too had been expecting me.

I crossed the fifty feet from the wall to the two massive doors. As I passed through the two doors for the first time, I noticed how old and immense they actually were. These appeared to be very ancient doors. They appeared to be about twenty-five feet tall. These doors were impeccably maintained and preserved even though they appeared to be ageless. Yet, as the angel closed the door it seemed to glide and hinged freely and silently. The thought came to me that there must be a wonderfully talented carpenter in this place. This amazed me and I stepped through into a very long hallway.

Inside the castle it was bright, yet there did not seem to be any light fixtures. The angel took a position to the right of the door and seemed to stand at attention. I looked down the hallway that seemed to be hundreds of feet long. The sound of the angelic worship was louder now, and the fragrance of frankincense and myrrh was tangible and thick in this place. The stones below my feet were cool and smooth, just like the ones outside. I turned once more to look at this angel; he seemed to be a gatekeeper. When I looked into the angels eyes, this scripture came into my mind: *"Bless the LORD, All you servants of the LORD, Who by night stand in the house of the LORD"* (Psalm 134:1). As this thought passed through my mind, the angel's smile brightened up and I realized that I should walk down the hall. As I moved on I noticed the height and breadth of the hallway, and I understood that even though it was just a hall it was also a very special place. The arched ceilings were very high and vaulted. The architecture in the stone castle was amazing.

Friends of God

As I strolled down the hall I started to notice shiny shields flanking me on each side of the walls. At first I thought that it was odd to see these shields displayed in the hallway. However, as I walked past one I began to realize that these were masterpieces. These shields were actually extremely valuable works of art. At once I understood that these shields were the actual shields of faith belonging to some of the Bible's greatest heroes and patriarchs. I saw the shield of King David. It was beautiful yet you can clearly see the dents and marks of battle. The shields of Gideon, Samuel, and Rahab were on display there.

I stopped and looked at some of these as I walked slowly down the hall. There were dozens, even hundreds of these shields of faith on display in this hallway. It also occurred to me that the majority of the shields that were on display were the shields of faith of God's friends. What was surprising to me was that many of the shields that were displayed were the shields of faith of men and women that the people of earth will never know. These are ordinary people whom the Lord treasures greatly.

You see, their faith is an actual substance and in the heavenly realms that is extremely valuable to the Lord (Hebrews 11:1). God takes great pleasure in the faith of ordinary men and women who place their trust and confidence totally in God. As this understanding bubbled up from within my spirit, I knew that this was an aspect of the rest of the Lord—trusting God. That is true faith. Such faith is pleasing to God the Father. In fact, without such faith it is impossible to please the Lord. Surely, God will reward such faith because that kind of faith is Kingdom faith. It is real, and it is tangible in the spiritual or heavenly realms (Hebrews 11:6). True faith is more valuable in heaven than platinum, gold, silver, or even fine gemstones like rubies and diamonds would be upon the earth. My stroll down this hallway of faith turned out to be an epiphany or "aha" moment.

I had been walking down the hallway observing these shields of faith for over an hour when I realized that I had only gone about one tenth of the way down the hall! In the center of the hallway ahead I could see a lot of light coming into the space from the right-hand side and I thought that the hall must be open to a court yard at that point. At that moment another angel stepped into the hallway and motioned for me to enter into a room on the left.

Stirring the Waters

When I stepped through the threshold of the door I realized that I had stepped into a magnificent bathroom. Unlike the hallway, the floors here were constructed of immaculate white marble as were the walls. The room was filled with brilliant light, what appeared to be sunshine flowed into the space through a large twelve-foot circular window that was set just behind the tub. The tub was also circular and also about twelve feet in circumference. Even the walls were constructed of white polished marble and this helped to magnify the glory and intensity of the light in the room.

In hindsight, I do not think that it was sunshine as we understand it upon the earth. Rather, it was the glory of God that was shining through. The sinks were also carved from a single piece of brilliant white marble. There was a crystal pitcher of water resting upon the marble sink. I entered and turned to the right to look at the circular window and the tub that was centered directly below it. The angel in attendance to this room was beautiful and smiled at me with acceptance. The angel's beautiful blue eyes also reflected the brilliant light in this room. The angel picked up the crystal pitcher and poured some of the crystal clear water into the tub and stirred the water.

The angel pointed at the tub and I noticed that it was nearly filled with crystal clear water. The water was exuding a wonderful aroma and it was apparent to me that the tub had been prepared especially for my visit. As the steam rose from the water in the tub it also emitted heavenly aromas of oils and healing agents that had been stirred into the water by the attendant angel. The scripture from John 5:4 came into my mind:

> *For an angel went down at a certain time into the pool and stirred up the water; then whoever stepped in first, after the stirring of the water, was made well of whatever disease he had.*

For the first time I realized that the robe that I was wearing was dirty and soiled. The angel motioned for me to remove it and left the room. Then I stepped into the tub and began to luxuriate in the warm, healing waters. The temperature was perfect, and the bath was a welcome and unexpected treat. I literally soaked in the waters for what seemed like hours. The fragrances were amazing and the water seemed to be treated with oils and was silky smooth to the touch. Once I accidentally splashed some of the water into my mouth and found that it tasted as wonderful as it smelled. The water had an effervescent quality and carried a touch of citrus scent in it. It was delightfully refreshing in more ways than one.

The Healing River

Through the massive circular window I could see the manicured gardens far below the beautiful stone castle. It occurred to me that this may have been the Father's house, but I was not sure. What I was sure of was that I as having was a wonderful relaxing and renewing time soaking in the perfumed waters. I rested my elbows upon the edge of the white tub and allowed my gaze to wonder out of the window onto the view below. In the distance I could see the river that flowed through the land. The thought occurred to me that this was the river of life that proceeded from the throne of God and from the throne of the Lamb (Revelation 22:1). Yet, as I observed the crystal clear river below I understood that it was the same healing river that Ezekiel saw flowing from under the door of the temple (Ezekiel 47:1-8).

Over the course of time as I soaked in the water of the tub and contemplated the heavenly landscape below I also realized that the river that I was seeing was the same still peaceful waters of Psalm 23 (v. 2). I thought about these things for what seemed like hours as I watched the sunshine reflect playfully off the pure river of the water of life, clear as crystal, proceeding from the throne of God and of the Lamb. I was surprised that my healing bath never seemed to cool down. It supernaturally remained at the optimum temperature. Somehow, as I soaked in this amazing tub in this supernatural bathroom I was being restored, cleansed, and healed. In fact, I would often return to this bathroom to be cleansed and restored before I would proceed out into the heavenly realms on future visits. After a while I turned over onto my back and rested in the Lord in the sweet smelling healing waters of the tub.

As a matter of fact, I actually drifted off into a restful sleep as I floated in the healing water. I dreamed about an angel handing me a towel and smiling at me with big blue eyes of understanding and compassion. When I woke up that same angel was standing at the edge of the tub with a large plush towel in hand. I took the towel and smiled at the angel. I rose up from the tub and stepped up out of the water and dried off with the fluffy white towel. The angel then placed a new immaculate robe upon me. I turned to look out of the circular window again, and a smile filled my face. Pure joy flowed through me at that instant and the cares of the world were forgotten. In my mind I thought: "It does not get any better than this."

I raised my left arm to look at my new garment. In the shimmering light of God's glory, the material glimmered in the light with a supernatural sheen and colors burst from it in all directions. I had never had a robe like this before! I left the bathroom and entered the hallway.

CHAPTER 12

The Great Banquet Hall

I turned to see the angel there wave goodbye and smile at me with tenderness. I started to walk down the hallway or what I had come to think of as the hall of faith. I walked past many more shields until I can to the opening in the hallway. When I reached it I found it full of light and glory. In this spot on the right-hand side of the hallway there was an extensive and ornate handrail fashioned of precious metals. It appeared that it was constructed of platinum, gold, and silver in a similar fashion to the gate at the entrance to the secret stairs. It had intricate patterns incorporated into the design, and the gold balusters, pickets, and post tops reflected the brilliance of the light of the glory entering into the room from above and below.

I was engrossed in observing this railing and did not notice the details of the hall below. I heard a sound echo from the ceiling to my left. Looking up I saw a man suspended upon a platform. In an instant I realized that he was an artist. It was then that I saw the magnificent frescos that adorned the ceiling of this great hall. The paintings that decorated the ceiling were incredible! The room below was massive and the paintings on the ceiling were also enormous. As I studied the massive murals and frescoes, I was amazed at the talent that must have been required to render such masterpieces.

Masterful Works of Art

The artwork in this massive room would make the Sistine Chapel and that of St. Peter's Cathedral appear to be the work of a mere amateur. What was more incredible was the quality of the paintings. The paintings that festooned these ceilings were of a higher quality that even Michael Angelo could have painted! The brilliance of the color palate and contrasts between the hues was superb! I was overwhelmed by the beauty and grandeur of the designs and the skill with which the frescos had been executed. My eyes were intoxicated by the beauty of the designs and paintings.

Suddenly the artist who was working spoke to me, saying, "Why don't you come up here and help me!" He had a brush in his hand as he had just finalized a tiny detail of the portrait that he had completed a second ago. He put the tiny detail brush down and turned to look at me, and I realized that this may have well have been Michael Angelo! I was stunned and stood in silence as I thought about the magnitude of the invitation to help this brilliant artist! My heart leapt and I realized that the artist's invitation was actually one of the desires of my heart.

I was speechless and stood there silently gazing at the sheer magnitude, breadth, and enormousness of this intricate work of art above my head. It must have taken centuries to complete! I relished looking at the murals for a long time. After a moment the artist smiled at me graciously and returned to his work. The frescoes and murals were astonishing and I was rendered speechless by the quantity and quality of the art that was suspended over my head. I was also astonished by the artist's invitation. The artist turned back to his work and I turned back to my thoughts. Perhaps this really was one of the hidden desires of his heart? For Michael Angelo this would be paradise!

Glory Explosion

From the corner of my eye I saw a flash of luminescent colors explode below me. I turned to look to my right and below, and that is when I saw Him. Jesus had just picked up a large crystal challis and the light had reflected from the liquid that was within the Lord's cup exploding in every direction. Jesus looked up at me and smiled. In that instant the glory of God enveloped me and I began to weep. Within my heart I ached to be with Jesus again. The Lord was seated at the far end of a very long banquet table. The massive table was about three hundred feet long and about eight feet wide. The table was adorned and set with the finest linens and china. It was surrounded by dozens of beautifully crafted high-backed chairs that were trimmed in gold. There was a smorgasbord of food upon the table, and it seemed that Jesus was waiting on someone before He was going to begin His meal.

Jesus looked up and our eyes met for a moment and I realized that the Lord was waiting for me! I looked behind me and saw l circular stairway leading to the massive hall below. I turned quickly and began to leap and run down the hallway was fast as I could manage. On the way down I noticed that the walls of the circular stairway were also lined with the shields of faith from the great cloud of witnesses. I made my way down three or four stories worth of stairs and rushed up to the two large arched wooden doors there. They were also hinged in gold and had golden handles in the center of each one. As I scampered across the hallway, an angel stepped forward and opened the door on my behalf. I ran into the great hall where the Lord was seated at the other end of a massive table.

For a moment I was frozen by the glory of God and fell to my knees weeping. It was so overcoming to be in the presence of Jesus again! Brilliant light and the glory of God filled the place. I found it difficult to move or even think at that instant. After a moment two angels moved to my side and helped me to stand. They smiled at me and gently raised me to my feet. I looked up to see the frescoes adorning the ceiling above and realized that the works of art there were even more spectacular than I had first understood. I took a moment to absorb the grandeur of the room realizing that I had been personally invited into the great banquet hall. I was surprised to see that it was totally empty save for Jesus and me. Even the artist was now gone, and only a few attendant angels remained in this place.

The room was massive and constructed of what seemed ancient architecture with great vaulting arches and ceilings around the circumference of the expanse of the enormous hall. Far above ornate windows admitted shafts of brilliant golden light which illuminated the banquet hall perfectly. Angelic worship filled the air along with fragrance of heaven. I looked to my left and saw hundreds of rows of long tables. Each table seemed to be over three hundred feet long, and they were all dressed out and with fine linens, silverware, and china. The banquet hall was prepared for a great supper (Revelation 19:9). I glanced at the Lord to see Him still smiling patiently at me, and with a sweeping gesture of His left hand He called me to Himself.

CHAPTER 13

The Feast

As I walked across of the expanse of the floor moving in the direction of Jesus, I could once again feel the coolness of the perfectly white marble floor under my bare feet. I could feel my beautiful white robe as it lightly dragged across the white marble floor. I finally entered in between two of the elongated tables and began to walk the remaining distance to the Lord who was seated at the head of the table on my right. The closer I came to the Messiah the more I realized and understood His unconditional love and incredible sacrifice for me. Great tears began to well up from within my spirit, and I began to weep as the presence of the Lord intensified as I approached Jesus. I noted that the table was made ready, the feast had been prepared, and the Messiah sat ready. Jesus is always ready! I wondered where the other guests were, but I was so overwhelmed by His presence that I lost that thought quickly.

When I came near the end of the table there were the four angels in attendance to Jesus. These were the same four angels that I have seen with the Lord before. The table had a fresh baked loaf of bread in the center of a silver serving tray. There were wine and crystal goblets for each of us. One of the angels pulled out a chair for me to sit down in at the right hand of Jesus. This was just too much for me! I fell down at the feet of

Jesus and began to weep as I received revelation and a small understanding of the magnitude of His sacrifice for me. I simply fell at the feet of Jesus and lay there. I wept. I wept for a long time until finally I felt the hand of the Lord upon my head and I heard the Lord say, "You are welcome here."

I placed my hands upon the Lord's feet and great tears poured from my eyes. This was my first invitation to join the Lord in the great banquet hall. I chose to lie at the feet of Jesus and worship Him. I wept for a very long time as waves of God's love and glory washed over me in rhythm to the angelic worship that filled the great hall. I just luxuriated in being at the feet of Jesus. Hours seemed to pass uninterrupted and I found myself back in my little prayer room at 121 Beech Street. I was unable to move for a long time and continued to weep as the tangible presence of the Lord pinned me to the old shag carpet. I understood that my life had been transformed by this encounter with Christ in the heavenly places.

Communion

On subsequent trips to the Father's house I would often repeat this process. I would walk along the stone pathway, and up to the balcony. I would enter into the same two massive and ancient doors and walk down the hall of faith. The white marble bathroom was always open and available for me to cleanse my body and soul there in. The beautiful angel was always present to hand me the fluffy white towel at the end of my soaking. I was always given a fresh and clean phosphorescent white robe to wear into the presence of Jesus. Over the course of time I noticed how the fresco on the ceiling of the great banquet hall was progressing and saw the artist moving across the upper heights of the great banquet hall as the ceiling was being adorned. I would often lie at the feet of Jesus weeping and luxuriating in this special place. On my second trip to the great banquet hall, the Lord placed His hand upon my head and told me to "arise and eat."

I did and the Lord and I partook of communion together many times in the great banquet hall. I would often sit with the Lord for communion. At those times the four angels would attend to our needs and pour the wine for the Lord and me. Jesus and I would often break bread together and enjoy meals jointly in the great banquet hall. We would pray and the Lord would lead us in taking the Lord's Supper. By the grace of God I have been able to experience communion with Jesus in the great banquet hall many times. After a season of visiting the Lord there, He began to invite me to visit other places in the realms of heaven. In the next several chapters I will describe some of those places to you the reader. I will also briefly outline what some of the Lord's angelic hosts are doing in the heavenly realms today.

CHAPTER 14

Entertaining Heaven

I pressed into the word of God all morning. The Lord had given me three scriptural confirmations on my last excursion into the heavenly realm. The Bible tells us that everything should be confirmed in the mouth of two or three witnesses (Matthew 18:16; 2 Corinthians 13:1). So I had asked the Lord for confirmation of the things that I had been seeing and experiencing in my visits to heaven.

It was a great pleasure to stay home and press into reading God's word and to invest time in the presence of the Holy Spirit as I prayed. Truly, I would rather do that than scrape lead-based paint from the old house that I was working on. Besides that it was too cold to paint and there was a chance of rain. So I locked the front door, unplugged the phone, and devoted the day to the Lord.

Since I had been traveling or ascending into heaven or the heavenly realms or places for the last few days, the presence and the anointing of the Holy Spirit seemed to have increased in my life. The glory and presence of the Lord was very tangible in the little house at 121 Beech Street. There was a residue of heaven in the little house, and many people discerned it. In fact, I was sure that angels were hanging around my little tabernacle. So I purposed in my heart to entertain them on purpose. I had read in the book of Hebrews that a person could entertain angels without being aware of it.

So in my mind, since angels had entertained me literally in the heavenly realms, I felt obligated to return the favor. After all, the angels had met me when I arrived. They had helped to give me a tour of the heavenly places (Ephesians 1:3, 20; 2:6). These angels had even helped to serve me fabulous food while I dined with Jesus in the great banquet hall. So it just seemed natural to me to make a point of blessing the Lord's angels here in my little home upon the earth! I made a conscious decision to entertain God's angels upon the earth, just as they have entertained me in the heavenly places. That just seemed like the right thing to do within my heart. Selah. When I began to entertain God's angels on the earth, it seems that the Lord, in His grace, allowed me to be entertained by His angels on the earth and in heaven!

Entertaining Angels

You know what? They responded almost immediately and I had many angelic encounters in the little house over the next two years. It was apparent to me that I had cracked or ripped open the heavens over the little house and it seemed that there was free access into the heavens there (Isaiah 64:1). I could go up, the Holy Spirit and God's angels could come down. Of course, the most important place where the Lord created an open heaven in this season was within my heart. I relaxed upon the bed in the little bedroom and studied and pondered the scriptures that Jesus had given me as confirmation. I had actually asked the Lord for confirmation and He told me to read

John 14 while I was in His presence in the heavenly places. I realized that God would confirm His word and His Kingdom in the mouths of two or three witnesses (2 Corinthians 13:1).

I had read John 14 before. But I never saw the fact that Jesus has actually gone ahead of me into heaven to prepare a place or abode for me. The Lord even said, *"I go to prepare place for you"* (v. 2) and, *"I will come again and receive you to Myself"* (v. 3). I found that amazing! When I read verses 1-3 I began to weep because I understood that these scriptures alone perfectly defined my previous visit to the great stone castle in the heavenly realm. Jesus said,

> *In My Father's house are many mansions; if it were not so, I would have told you. I go to prepare a place for you. And if I go and prepare a place for you, I will come again and receive you to Myself; that where I am, there you may be also. And where I go you know, and the way you know.*

I could not believe my eyes when I first read this. Houses in heaven! And what was more they are built by God for me. There are houses in heaven that are also built for you too! The Lord was giving us an invitation to be where He is. And it is certain that Jesus is now in heaven and we can be with Him there too (John 3:3; Ephesians 4:8-9).

His Good Treasure

I had never thought about the fact that a person did not need die to be with Jesus in heaven. I had never heard that preached in church. In the Book of Malachi I saw where the Bible speaks about how God will open the windows of heaven. I thought,

"That is exactly what I am experiencing! God has opened the heavens over me and He is pouring out blessings upon me in this little place." Deuteronomy 28:12 speaks of this character and grace of giving supernatural blessings of the Lord: *"The LORD will open to you His good treasure, the heavens...."* In my heart I never wanted to leave the little disheveled house. It was heaven on earth to me. The scriptures in Malachi also referred to a book of remembrance which was written before God (v. 16). That made me think, and I remembered how I had seen angels writing in what appeared to be books in the heavenly places. Of course, God has angels who write! The Apostle John said that he saw so many millions of angels in heaven that it was impossible for him to comprehend their number or to count them.

In John 14 quoted above Jesus speaks of "My Father's house" and "many mansions." Jesus also told us that He was the "way" to the Father's mansions (v. 6). Since these events transpired nearly two decades ago, I have had a lot of time to pray and seek the Lord about them. I have meditated upon what I experienced, and I have pondered them in my heart consistently. Assuredly I say to you that I was reluctant to share them at all. I consider these heavenly experiences holy "kisses" of heaven.

I have asked the Lord what I was really experiencing and where exactly I was "taken" to in these "heavenly experiences." It is possible that the large stone castle or home that I visited in the heavens was actually my heavenly mansion or home. However, it is also possible that I also visited the actual Father's house on numerous occasions (John 14:2). I believe that I was actually in heaven during these experiences (weather in body of out of body I am not certain).

The words, "Father's house," found in John 14 can be literally translated from the Strong's Greek Concordance # G3614, as *oikia*, meaning properly a residence or home (abstractly), but usually (concretely) an abode (literally or figuratively); referring to an actual structure or building, and by implication the property of a single family (especially domestics): - home, house (-hold).

It is possible that Jesus is referring to our heavenly inheritance as an engrafted child of God (see Romans 11; 8:14, 19; 9:26; Galatians 3:26; and 4:6). We are a valuable part of God's extended family. We are sons and daughters of God. You are a "joint heir" with Christ, who has a supernatural inheritance laid up for you in the heavenly realms. Personally, I find this quite exciting, and I hope that this book will spark your interest and passion to press into the Kingdom of God and receive your heavenly inheritance. Remember, you need not die to visit heaven.

The Bible clearly teaches and illustrates that we have a real home to look forward to in heaven when we die and depart from this earth or temporal realm. Our spirits will live on for eternity with Christ in the realms of heaven. That is provided that we believe that Jesus Christ is our Messiah, or Savior, and we choose to accept God's offer of free salvation. Entering heaven is conditional and we must choose it. Jesus uses the Greek word *monē* in John 14 saying that there are "many mansions" in His Father's house, or in heaven. The Greek word *monē* is similar to *oikia*; again, meaning a place to stay, a residence, an abode or mansion. (See Strong's Greek Concordance reference #G3306.)

Finally, when the Lord says that He would go and prepare "a place" for us, He is referring to a spot (generally in space, but limited by occupancy that is, location as a position, home, tract of land, etc.). (See Strong's Greek Concordance reference #G5117.) Jesus is saying that He is giving to us or preparing for us an excellent opportunity, or specifically a legal or licensed place, quarter, room, or building that we may occupy freely.

Those who choose Christ's salvation and heaven will not be required to toil to pay rent. There will be no mortgages in our heavenly homes. Nor will we be required to till the ground to grow the food that we will eat. We will not be nourished by our own labors or the sweat of our brows. The implication is paradise or heaven. Paul the Apostle was "taken up" or "caught up" into the realms of heaven and reportedly "saw paradise." There is actually quite a bit of biblical evidence for these kinds of heavenly encounters or supernatural experiences. There are numerous examples of this throughout the Bible. Therefore the kinds of experiences that are illustrated in this book are thoroughly biblical (see 2 Corinthians 12:1-3, Ezekiel 1:1, Revelation 4:1, Genesis 28:12, and Genesis 32:2 ,to name but a few).

In Revelation 5:11 John testified: *"I looked, and I heard the voice of many angels around the throne, the living creatures, and the elders; and the number of them was ten thousand times ten thousand, and thousands of thousands."* It made perfect sense to me now. All of those millions of books that I had been seeing in the Father's library were very scriptural. Then I understood why Jesus had told me to read in Revelation 20:12 about books in heaven:

> *I saw the dead, small and great, standing before God, and books were opened. And another book was opened, which is the Book of Life. And the dead were judged according to their works, by the things which were written in the books.*

If God will open every individual's books of life upon the earth, there must surely be millions upon millions of books in heaven.

Scientific studies suggest that approximately 108 billion **people have born upon the earth.[1] As of this writing it is estimated that over seven and a half billion people inhabit the planet.[2]** Imagine all of those books of life! As I meditated upon these things that day, I was actually stunned and lay upon my bed praising the Lord and thanking Him for the privilege that He was giving me to ascend into the Father's house. I thanked the Lord and within my heart a desire to return to the Lord's presence was birthed. So I had an internal desire to thank the Lord personally. By the time I had finished reading and thinking about everything that I had experienced over the last few months, it was well into the afternoon.

CHAPTER 15

Millions of Angels

It was cold and grey outside, and I decided to take another hot bath. I filled the tub again and soaked in the presence of the Lord for a long time. When I finished I got dressed and stepped into the bedroom to comb my hair. As I was looking at myself in the mirror on the door, the Lord spoke to me saying, "Kevin, come up here." I leaped into my prayer closet again and positioned myself upon the floor to pray. This is often how I pray. I just lie down and rest or luxuriate in the presence of the Lord in the same way that I do when I lie at Jesus' feet in the heavenly places. You should try it sometime. This kind of prayer can be life changing in ways that I do not fully understand. One minute in the real presence and glory of God can transform your life forever. Learn to rest in His glory!

Some call this "soaking" prayer, but really it is just waiting upon the Lord or resting in the Lord. I would purpose in my heart to still or quiet my carnal mind. I would try to keep my mind and emotions from running in all directions. I would bring my thoughts into captivity (2 Corinthians 10:5). I discovered that it was helpful to pray in the Holy Spirit when seeking to subdue my thoughts. Praying in the Spirit helped to bring my mind into subjection to my spirit. From this point I could perceive the voice of the Lord and comprehend supernatural things more easily. I was exercising my spiritual senses and also working on developing my spiritual discernment as well (Hebrews 5:14; 1 Corinthians 2:14). I prayed for a while and gave the Lord thanksgiving. I allowed my prayers to go up with praise, and I began to give the Lord thanks for allowing me to have the visits to be with Him in heaven. I began to thank the Lord for allowing me to return to Him again. After a few moments I could feel the familiar sensation of my spirit rising up.

For the third day in a row I positioned myself in the little prayer closet and began to earnestly pray. It is important to be diligent in prayer at times. Almost immediately I was launched heavenward, and I smiled as I understood that I was being allowed to come to Jesus in the heavens again. I landed on the stone pathway again. The same two angels were there to greet me and cushion my landing. It seemed that they had been expecting me. I once again vaulted up the secret stairs to enter into the Father's house. I paid little attention to the beautiful gardens below the crystal clear river that flowed in the distance, but I could smell the flowers and plants as I ran up the stone stairs. The angelic doorkeeper smiled at me as I breezed past him and bolted into the bathroom to be cleansed. I was given yet another new robe from the angelic attendant there. Once again I was in awe of the translucence of the material and smoothness of the robe.

"Praise the Lord"

I flew down the hallway of faith and ran down the circular stairway leading to the great banquet hall. Entering the great banquet hall I looked for Jesus. He was seated at our usual table, and once again He waved at me. I threw both hands up and shouted loudly, "Praise the Lord!" My words echoed through the massive vaulted ceiling, and I saw a couple angels turn from their chores to smile at me. I ran to Jesus as fast as my feet could carry me. As I entered into the presence of Jesus, I was overcome as the power and love of the Messiah washed over me in waves. When I reached the Lord I fell upon my face at the Lord's feet once more to worship Jesus. I just luxuriated in the glory of God at the Lord's feet for a long time that afternoon. I just wanted to be with Him.

After some time one of the four angels helped me to stand, and I sat down in the place that had been prepared for me. Jesus and I broke bread together again, and we laughed and smiled at one another during our time in the great banquet hall. I thanked the Lord and talked to Him about many of the things that were upon my heart that day. Later the Lord arose and walked purposely to the hidden door in the great banquet hall. We walked down the hallway and into the reading room preceded by the other four angelic beings that always accompanied the Lord and me. The Lord took up His usual position in His reading chair. The four angels took up their place and the two guardian angels in the reading room were there to greet me with a stern smile again. I took a moment to scan the room again.

CHAPTER 16

A Heavenly Place: The Vault of Spare Body Parts

As it turned out, I was able to visit this area of the Father's house on numerous occasions. It seemed that each time that I would enter the reading room the Lord would allow me to learn something new and exciting about His Kingdom. So as I walked around inspecting the room more closely, I was also wondering what He would show or reveal to me this afternoon. I also noticed that even though the room and its contents were obviously ancient, there was no dirt or dust. In fact, when I reflected upon this I realized that I had not seen any dirt in any of the rooms of the great, grey, stone mansion that I had been visiting. This thought brought a smile to my face and I leaned over to pick up the edge of my white robe and inspect it. It was perfectly clean too. Amazing, I thought, "Heaven is perfectly clean!" Later I would understand that it is one of the duties of God's angelic host to keep the heavenly realms clean and perfectly maintained.

As these thoughts were percolating in my mind, the Lord called me to Himself and instructed me to follow the two guardian angels. As He was saying this, the two angels approached the Lord and acknowledged His command with a slight bow. Jesus pointed to one of the vault doors on the southeast section of the reading room. The two angels then escorted me over to the vault, walking at a deliberate pace. When we reached the vault door I found it to be similar to the other one that I had seen the captain guardian angel open the day before. This vault door was the same size. It was immense and was also fashioned of heavy metals and appeared to be platinum.

The captain or leader of these two strong angels stepped forward again and commenced to work and manipulate the various wheels and knobs that protruded from the face of this vault. I could once again see the fire crackling in the ornate fireplace in the reading room reflecting from the highly polished metal of the door. There was the sound of clicking, and I could hear bearings and the mechanism of the vault door as they began to open under the angels hands. I heard the same sound of a hermetic seal being broken and air rushed past my head again. Only this time the smell of the air was more sterile in aroma. This surprised me and as the door opened bright light flooded into the reading room. The two guardian angels took up positions on the left and right of the open vault door to reveal an opening about fifteen feet wide and about twenty-four feet tall.

You Are Welcome Here

I looked at the inside of the massive door and I realized that it was nearly three feet thick. I was looking at the mechanisms of the door when a voice interrupted my inspection: "You are welcome in this place." I looked up to see another pair of normal-sized angels standing at the entrance to the vault door. These two angels were shorter than the other two guardian

A Heavenly Place: The Vault of Spare Body Parts

angels. These two angels had beautiful white wings and were only slightly taller than I am. They were very handsome and fine-looking; both had long curly blond hair. They stepped aside in unison making a space for me to enter into the area behind the door. As I stepped through the opening, I realized that I was entering into a storage area. Immediately I knew that the room was sterile. And it had the appearance and atmosphere of a medical facility.

The two angels seemed to be very excited that I was entering the sealed room. Somehow, I understood that other people had been here before me, but I also felt that it had been a while since the two angels had received a visitor. The angel who seemed to be the leader of the two spoke to me then saying, "Please feel free to look around. This place will always be here in your times of need." This statement struck me as a little funny, and I did not understand what the angel meant by this. Slowly I walked further into the room. Because of the seemingly sterile environment, I was hesitant to touch anything. I thought, "I need to be careful and not contaminate these books and other things." I saw what appeared to be instruction manuals stacked and arranged very carefully in that area. When this thought came into my mind, the angel who had spoken to me said, "You need not be concerned. You are welcome here and may have whatever you wish from this place." This really surprised me and gave me pause.

Whatever You Need

The reason for this was because of the items that were stored so methodically here. Before me were endless rows of neatly arranged shelves. They were perhaps fifty feet tall and each row as perhaps a hundred yards long. There were literally hundreds of rows of shelves. Upon each shelve was what appeared to be stainless steel containers of various sizes. There were also what appeared to be crystal clear jars or vessels. There must have been millions upon millions of these.

Each stainless steel tray held human body parts. At first this caused me to be a little alarmed. Once again the angel said, "You need not be concerned. You are welcome here and may have whatever you wish from this place." When He said that for the second time, revelation began to well up from my spirit. This was the vault of spare body parts, and these spare body parts would be released to people upon the earth who needed them. This understanding was astounding and overwhelmed my mind, and I began to smile broadly. At that moment the angel said, "You may have whatever you need from this place. Please look at these and touch them if you wish. You are welcome here."

With the angels permission I began to look at the body parts more carefully. There were fingers, hands, thumbs, tips of fingers, arms, legs, ears, noses, and other exterior body parts in one section. In another I saw inner ears, eyeballs, veins, arteries, and nerves arranged and cataloged in a precise and very neat order. The eyeballs were stored in pairs or as individual units, each in their own crystal jar or vessel. In another section I saw skeletal parts, and various bones and parts of the skeleton. In another section I saw organs. There were hearts, livers, lungs, kidneys, bladders, intestines, and so on. I remember thinking that there are a lot of people back on earth that could really use these. In another section I saw containers that were filled with volumes of blood and what appeared to be bone marrow. Somehow I knew that these items held the key for the healing of many people upon the earth who are battling AIDS/HIV as well as for other incurable blood diseases upon the earth.

Perfectly Formed

When this thought came into my mind, the angel said, "Freely you have received, freely you may give" (Matthew 10:7-8). This also bewildered me to a great extent, and I continued my tour of this wing of the library. I took the stainless steel containers down and looked at legs that appeared to belong to infants and toddlers. As I touched these items I understood that these were body parts for children who were afflicted with paralytic diseases upon the earth. There were perfectly formed infant hands and feet too. These arms, legs, fingers, toes, and lips in heaven could be the key to their healing. I picked up jars that had various colored eyes and I was intrigued as I looked into the eyes in these jars. I wondered who these were meant for, and I realized that there were people who literally needed to have a new eye or pair of eyes upon the earth. It was a little strange to hold an eyeball and have it stare back at you from the jars. I was surprised when I noticed that the pupils of the eyes in the crystal containers seemed to dilate when I looked at them.

I held hearts which seemed to be ever so slightly beating in my hands. I looked though the vault for hours until it occurred to me that I needed to return the Lord in the reading room.

By then I had twisted and turned up and down many rows of these shelves and I realized that I could no longer see the door to the reading room. I carefully placed a small infant's heart back upon the shelves in front of me in its specified place and looked around to my right. I wondered, "How am I going to get out of here?" At that instant the angel tapped me upon my left shoulder and said, "Follow me." I followed the angel and his associate through the maze of aisles of shelves. In a few moments I saw the entrance and the vault door.

As I was preparing to leave, the angel waved good-bye to me and repeated, "You are always welcome here. You may have whatever you wish from this place." The angel waved and smiled graciously at me as I prepared to step back through the door. I waved back to this angel. For an instant our eyes locked and I realized that this angel was free to deliver any of the body parts that I had seen to individuals on earth. I thought, "I hope I see these guys someday back upon the earth." When this thought crossed my mind, both angels began to smile broadly as if to confirm that I would be seeing them in the future. I walked through the door and watched as the two guardian angels closed the vault and once again sealed it with mechanisms that I did not comprehend. There was a "whoosh" of air, and I turned to see Jesus just as He put down a large book that He had been reading. He smiled at me and motioned for me to join Him.

CHAPTER 17

Working with Angels of Healings and Creative Miracles

When I reached the Lord He was also smiling broadly. As I sat down, He said, "The two angels that you saw are anointed to work with my servants upon the earth. There are many more of my angelic servants like the two that you met today. From now on they will be available to assist you as you pray for my people. They can work with you to release creative miracles to those who need creative miracles in their bodies. At times they will be released to co-labor with my friends as they are anointed with the gifts of healings and miracles. Remember what you have seen and heard here today. The time is coming when my people will be released to minister in the gifts of miracles and healings in a new and greater level. My angels, like the ones that you just saw, will play a role in the release of these gifts of the Holy Spirit. Prepare yourself for this, and when the time is right I will open the door for you to tell my people to be ready for this."

The Lord and I spoke about angels and creative miracles for a bit more. After a while Jesus seemed to be satisfied that I understood Him clearly, and then the Lord stood up and we left the reading room and took a walk out into the gardens. As we walked I pondered in my heart the things that I had seen and heard. Later in 2002 I had an opportunity to begin to work with healing angels like the two that I met in the vault of body parts. Angels like the two in the vault help to release creative miracles, and many of these kinds of God's angels are available for anyone to work with today. That includes everyone who is reading this now. God's angels like this are released by simple faith of God's people and through the spoken word of the Lord (Luke 1:37; Psalm 103:20).

You can co-labor with God's angels to release creative miracles. During a missions' trip in 2003, a team that I was leading and I prayed for a man named Leonard who grew a new eyeball. That well documented creative miracle was a direct result of angelic ministry released through angelic beings like the two that I met in the vault of body parts. That testimony is outlined in the book *Visitations of Angels and Other Supernatural Experiences Volume #2*. Healing angels like this have also played a role in releasing creative miracles through my ministry consistently for nearly two decades.

Recently I have experienced several instances where the Lord has allowed me to pray and release or activate the angels that have access to the vault of spare body parts. In May of 2017 we prayed for a toddler named Angel. She was born with a deformed heart. The doctors had instructed her father that she needed a very complicated heart surgery. They also told the father that there was a very small percentage of her surviving the complicated surgery.

Angel's father contacted us and requested that we pray and intercede for his daughter. As I was going into my prayer room on Saturday, I simple prayed to the Father and asked in Jesus' name to loose His angel from the room or vault of spare body parts to minister to Angel. On Monday Angel was being prepped for the surgery; but in the end that doctor approached Angel's father telling him, "We do not know what has happened, but there is no need for the surgery. Angel's heart has grown new veins and arteries and there is new tissue that has appeared. It appears that Angel's heart has healed itself." We have seen literally hundreds of miracles like these as we have learned to entertain heaven and co-labor with the Holy Spirit to re-create Christ in our lives. You can too.

There have been many other times that the Lord has allowed me to work in pray in this way. We have seen internal organs recreated or healed and eyeballs grow back. Recently we have witnessed many people who were short in stature actually grow in height. One woman from Ohio grew an estimated four and one-half inches and was able to drive normally for the first time in her life. If you would like to read more testimonies like these there are dozens of testimonies posted on our Web page at http://kingofgloryministries.org/index.php/writings/index/testimonies/.

In the next chapter I begin to share several testimonies which describe other areas of heaven including Psalm 23, the Lord's manicured gardens, and the fountain of living waters.

CHAPTER 18

The River of Revelation

Tonight, just a few minutes ago, the Lord spoke to me. It is not unusual for Jesus to speak to me like this. Sometimes I am allowed to enter into the realms of heaven. The Lord sometimes invites me into His very presence. Many times I have dined with Jesus in the great banquet hall. Sometimes Jesus invites me to explore the different rooms and places in His Father's great mansion. (See John 14:2.) The Lord has also been allowing me to explore the vast areas and lands that are surrounding the beautiful stone mansion and its manicured gardens.

There are hundreds of thousands of square miles in this beautiful heavenly land about the glorious home that Jesus is allowing me to tour. One of my most favorite places to go is the beautiful green meadows by the still crystal clear waters. One of my favorite things to do in that place is to simply lie at the feet of Jesus. We usually do this after dinner in the great banquet hall. I will ask Jesus to allow me to sit with Him by the still waters and listen to His sayings or just luxuriate in His glory. We will leave the banquet hall and walk down a great winding grey stone walkway that leads to the gardens and fountains of life therein. We are always accompanied by four friendly angels who serve the Lord and see to our needs by ministering to us in various ways.

I often ask the Lord to go to the still waters by the crystal river of God. There the angels will have prepared a place for us. There is a beautiful blanket or ornate quilts waiting for us. I lie at the feet of Jesus on one quilt and bask in the heavenly sunshine. The Lord will speak to me and I just listen quietly to His sayings. In this place I am totally content just being in the presence of Jesus.

The still waters are the waters of life. These are the very still waters of Psalm 23, and they flow crystal clear and silently through the heart of this heavenly place. They flow proceeding from the throne of God and of the Lamb that is found in the crystal cathedral in heaven. (See Revelation 22:1.) They are the waters of the river in the Garden of Eden. They are the healing waters of Ezekiel 47. They are the healing waters of Psalm 23. They are the healing waters of Revelation 22. They are the waters of Psalm 46. They are the waters of Numbers 20:11. This beautiful crystal clear water meanders by the fruitful meadows in the place Psalm 23. The Lord has allowed me to free dive into the crystal clear depths of the river of life.

This river of life is clear and warm. Beside the banks of this river grow beautiful trees of all kinds, and they are always bearing fruit. These trees are always in full bloom, and they also have ripe fruit at all times. The trees provide for the needs of the people in this wonderful place. These perfect trees are beautiful beyond compare and they always release a wonderful heavenly aroma. The sensation you get when you smell their fragrance is like the feeling you get when your mom takes a fresh baked hot apple pie out of the oven. Your mouth begins to water and your spirit begins to soar when you behold the beauty and fragrance of these trees. There are thousands upon thousands of trees like this that line the river of life in this heavenly place. (See Revelation 22:2.)

Hidden Mysteries

In the river of life I have made many discoveries. There I have found treasures. Jesus has allowed me to keep many of these heavenly things. Once, Jesus Himself swam with me in the still waters of the river of life. On the dive I showed the Lord a sunken treasure chest that I had discovered on a previous expedition. The treasure chest rests in about seventy foot of water near a bend in the river of life, and is full of treasures. It has thousands of precious gemstones and other articles that are hidden in the chest.

When Jesus free dove with me He chose a very large and multifaceted diamond for me from the depths of the sunken chest. It was a brilliant crystal clear. When we inspected the diamond in the radiant sunshine of the Psalm 23 meadow, a cascade of colors radiated from this perfectly cut heavenly gem. When Jesus would rotate the gem in His right hand, between His thumb and forefinger, the gemstone would send arrays of luminous colors throughout the area, and revelation seemed to flow into my spirit instantaneously. At other times I have taken jewels from the hidden trove, but none have been as magnificent as the one that Jesus gave to me. Once I found a small diamond and another time I found a very small but brilliant red ruby.

When I show these heavenly gemstones to Jesus, He always seems to give me some new revelation. On another occasion when I was diving with Jesus in the river of life, He directed me to a small pouch. I somehow knew that the pouch was very ancient and was a coin purse. It is about the size of my hand and is closed by a leather band. The Lord is using these things to reveal to me some of the hidden treasures of heaven and His Kingdom. (See Proverbs 25:2.) When the Lord gave me the coin purse, Jesus and I ascended back up through the crystal clear waters about seventy feet to the surface of the waters of life. When we arrived at the shore the four angels were waiting for us with two immaculate white towels and the angels helped us to dry ourselves off. Then we returned to our beautiful quilts and sat in the warming sunshine.

I have seen these angels many times before. These are the same four angels that were with Jesus when He called me to come to Him in heaven the first time. I know them. They are gentle and meek and walk in humility much like Christ. The first one that I was introduced to has beautiful blond hair, which is shoulder length. This angel has bright piercing blue eyes. Jesus has allowed me to work with this angel before in order to see my prayers answered. That is an amazing feeling when Jesus allows you to loose an angel and then you see the results of the answered prayers bringing needed things, or healing, or revelation and such!

Later, Jesus took the purse from me and showed me the "combination" needed to open it. He handed it to me smiling and with a great deal of satisfaction. It seemed that the Lord was very happy to be giving these heavenly treasures away. When I looked inside the pouch I discovered that it contained twelve perfect diamonds. They were identical in shape, clarity, and cut. The diamonds were perfect and spotless. Somehow I knew that these represented Christ's spotless Bride. The diamonds were about the size of a man's thumb, and would be extremely valuable on earth. Priceless!

CHAPTER 19

The Sword of the Lord

I have found other treasures in the river of life. These include a beautiful two-edged sword. This sword fit my hand as if it had been tailor-made for my grip. The sword of the Lord is of the finest workmanship, and fashioned of the finest gold. The blade has fine inlaid work and is obviously of heavenly manufacture. It is light as a feather and as sharp as a laser. The Lord has instructed me to use this weapon of warfare in the prayer ministry and in intercession on occasion. I understand that the sword of the Lord would be used as a great blessing in my life as time passed.

The Holy Spirit will often lead me to unsheathe the sword to cut off hindrances from those whom I have prayed for. I have used the sword to surgically remove generational curses and associated demonic spirits. The sword of the Lord is especially effective when it is used in this manner. Spirits of infirmity and the spirit of death and suicide are loosed as the sword cuts and frees. At other times it will be used to dismember demonic beings, breaking their assignments and freeing people in various ministry settings and places on earth.

On another occasion I also found a beautiful small golden dagger. It has a large round ruby encased in the end of its handle. This is a spiritual weapon of warfare, and I know that it has been hidden for many centuries. The Lord will give His people many of these kinds of powerful weapons in the coming season. (See 2 Corinthians 10:4.)

On the day that Jesus gave me the twelve perfect diamonds, He started to show me things in His Kingdom. I stayed at the feet of Jesus for a long time that afternoon by the still waters of Psalm 23. We allowed the gentle breeze to dry our hair and the white robes that we were wearing. The Lord was glad that I was near Him and allowed me to lie at His feet for a long time. I soaked in the presence of Jesus adoring the Lamb of God. I could smell the wonderful heavenly fragrance of the Lord. The fragrance of His presence smells like a mixture frankincense and roses. I could also smell the fragrance of the flora and fauna that grows in abundance beside the river of life—heaven.

CHAPTER 20

Jesus Loves the Little Children

Luke 18:15-17 (KJV):

And they brought unto him also infants, that he would touch them: but when his disciples saw it, they rebuked them. But Jesus called them unto him, and said, Suffer little children to come unto me, and forbid them not: for of such is the kingdom of God. Verily I say unto you, Whosoever shall not receive the kingdom of God as a little child shall in no wise enter therein.

This morning I experienced this passage of Scripture! As I was praying in my little prayer closet, the Lord appeared to me in a vision. I saw Jesus again. He was beckoning me to come to Him. I saw the Lord with His hands outstretched. The Lord was waving at me, and He was motioning me to ascend into the heavens with Him. So I went! The instant that I purposed in my heart to go to the Lord, I was lifted up and felt as if I was leaving my body. I found my spirit soaring into the heavenly places. This experience usually lasts for several minutes. When I landed I found myself surrounded by angels. I know these four angels and I have seen them before.

The angels caught me as I landed, and then they helped me to stand. It took a moment for me to get my balance. So the angels held me firmly but gently by my arms. As I looked at them they smiled and seemed to reassure me that everything was okay. I looked to my left and saw an angel that I know. His beautiful blue eyes sparkled with love and grace. He smiled at me and continued to hold me up.

I began to smell the wonderful fragrances of this place. Floral aromas and grasses abound here. I looked down at the stone pavers under my bare feet. They felt cool and smooth. I looked ahead and saw an ornate bed of manicured flowers that seemed to be worshiping Jesus. It seemed that I could almost hear their beauty. I was filled with love and peace. I was so pleased to be in this place again. I glanced at the crystal blue sky and saw wispy clouds dancing by. I took another deep breath and inhaled paradise again. The angel on my right let loose of his grip and motioned to the meadow nearby.

When I looked in that direction, I saw the Lord. He was waiting for me in our usual spot. The angels had prepared a place for us. There was a small serving table and our beautiful quilts were laid side by side. Tenderly I broke free from my angelic friends' grip and ran to the Lord. I was again overcome with the power of His unconditional love and began to weep. Jesus smiled at me and welcomed me into His arms of Love. I luxuriated in the arms of Christ and wept for a long time. Time seemed to stand still, and I could smell the pungent fragrance of fresh baked bread in His immaculate white robe. I inhaled again and relished the fragrance of God.

Then the Lord spoke to me and said, "I love those who love Me, And those who seek Me early will find Me. True riches and honor are with me, enduring riches and righteousness are found in Me. My fruit is better than gold, yes, than fine gold, and My revenue than choice silver. I traverse and walk the way of righteousness, and I move in the midst of the paths of justice. I will cause those who love Me to inherit wealth, and I will fill their treasuries with real riches." Then the Lord peeled me away from His embrace and looked deeply into my eyes. Such beautiful eyes! Christ's eyes are so rich and loving. He held me at arm's length with both hands upon my shoulders, and indicated that we should sit in the place that was prepared for us. What a wonderful time, and what a beautiful portrait of Christ.

In this lovely region of Psalm 23, there are a profusion of flowers. There are so many different varieties of flowers that I cannot begin to name them all. Somehow I know that there are varieties of flowers in this heavenly place that do not grow on earth. But there are also some of the most beautiful roses and majestic sunflowers that I have ever seen. I have also knelt on my hands and knees gazing at the most spectacular purple lilies of the field in the meadows of Psalm 23. The aroma that these tiny ethereal flowering plants produce is truly mesmerizing and actually intoxicating. There is a rainbow of colors that these teeny little flowers grow into. Each color seems to have its own distinctive heavenly fragrance.

I have observed that as the Lord Jesus walks past these flowers that they actually turn and bend towards the Son of God just as flowers on earth turn to face the sun in the heavens too. The flowers seem to worship the Christ as He passes by. Even the grass seems to worship the Savior. Occasionally a gentle breeze or zephyrs will flow through Psalm 23, and when this happens it seems that even the trees worship Jesus as they appear to "clap their leaves." Even the stones seem to cry out and worship the Lord in this incredible place. (See Isaiah 55:1.)

When we sat down on the magnificent quilts, the sounds and perfume of heaven invaded my senses in a fresh new way. I was lost in the wonder and the majesty of God's creation. The still crystal clear river meandered slowly by. It seemed that it had an eternity to reach its destination. By the bank of the river, flowering trees swayed and seemed to be worshiping God. They emitted a bouquet of heavenly fragrances. Flowers of innumerable variety also danced and swayed in the gentle breeze. I looked at the small table between us. It was ornately and expertly crafted and inlaid with silver and gold patterns. It held a fresh baked loaf of bread, fruit, and a crystal carafe of wine. Jesus took a loaf of bread and blessed it, giving the Father thanks for it this day. Then He broke a small piece off and handed it to me. When I took it from His right hand, I saw the nail scars and tears began to form in my eyes. Jesus smiled again and with His left hand put His index finger to his lips, signaling me to cease. So I wiped the tears from my eyes on the back of my right hand and took the bread from the Lord with my left hand.

An angel stepped up and poured red wine into a golden goblet that was intended for me. I tasted the bread and was amazed at the richness and goodness of its flavor. Setting my bread on the little serving table, I took the goblet and tasted the wine. It was rich and strong. It seemed that the flavor penetrated through every fiber of my being. At that instant a short gust of wind blew my hair around, and I could hear the laughter of little children being carried upon the breeze. These children were singing and laughing with glee. I cocked my head to the side and listened to the melody for a moment. I noticed that Jesus was also listening and was smiling with delight. I looked down the meadow and saw the beautiful sunlight reflecting off the still waters as they meandered by. The light there seemed to create a cascade of rainbow colors in the air as the sun filtered through the shimmering cirrus clouds above.

Butterflies flitted around the flowers and seemed to hover around the Lord. I watched them in amazement, as they would from time land upon His shoulder for a moment. The butterflies seemed to gently touch Him with their colorful wings before taking flight again. It seemed to be an act of worship. When I had finished my bread and wine, I lay down on the quilt at the feet of Jesus. The Lord was sunning His bare feet in the warm air. I listened to His sayings for a long time, just taking pleasure being in His presence and hearing His sweet voice. Christ's voice is like music to my ears, much like a symphony of excellent harps and soothing woodwinds or the sounds of many soothing waters.

I was simultaneously enjoying the fragrances of the flowers and trees. It seemed that honeysuckle and jasmine lingered in the crisp clean air. Other delicate scents mingled with these, but I was not aware of what they were. They smelled wonderful to breathe in and inhale. The fragrances seemed to be alive, and it seemed that I could actually taste the fragrances of heaven today.

CHAPTER 21

The Greatest in the Kingdom of Heaven

I watched as one of the butterflies flew further up into the green pasture. It was a brilliant purple. For some reason I was drawn to this particular butterfly. After a while I saw the group of small children that I had heard singing previously. One little girl began to chase the brilliant purple butterfly around and around. However, the butterfly seemed to flitter just out of the little one's reach eluding her hands. Each time the little girl would swoon and giggle as she reached out for the floating creature. I closed my eyes for a few minutes and luxuriated in Jesus' presence and in His sayings. I was reveling in the joyous carefree laughter of little children that was reaching me from a distance.

After a time, the cheerful sound of laughter filled my ears. The laughter was pure and full of joy. It filled my ears with delight and pleasure. I propped myself up on my right elbow to watch these children play and laugh so merrily. It was at that moment that I saw dozens of little children running. They all seemed to be in pursuit of the little girl with long curly blond hair who was still seeking diligently to catch the brilliant purple butterfly. For the first time I noticed that several angels were also running with these children. At that instant it occurred to me that these angels were the children's friends and caretakers. Jesus also sat up and looked around to His left saying, "Here they come! They are coming here!" This seemed to give the Lord great pleasure and satisfaction.

The large group of children ran up and began to play beside the Lord and me. The Lord rose up and began to dance, sing, and play with the children. At that moment the children jumped upon Jesus and they all tumbled over with a plop! Jesus began to laugh with the children, and it seemed that He never wanted to stop. They all began to play together on the grassy meadow. Jesus was full of laughter, smiles, and delight. The children formed a big circle and Jesus joined hands with two of them and they all began to spin around and around. I realized that Jesus often plays with the children in this way. I jumped up and joined the children and their angels in the dance. Soon I was laughing and filled with delight. Occasionally we would all tumble down together and Jesus would wrestle with the children on the grass, laughing all the while.

Laughing with Jesus

I returned to the blankets and observed them for some time. Jesus loves the little children, and He was so happy to be in their presence. They smiled and laughed as they played Ring Around the Rosie. After a time I joined them again and we all danced by the river of life. We were dancing and laughing with Jesus. Even the angels joined in our circle and danced with us singing and praising God! While we danced and laughed the bright green clover tickled between my toes as we played in our bare feet. What a happy and joyful time that was. This was one of the first times that I had danced with angels. Even though I danced so hard, there were no grass stains on my feet when we sat back down. I was surprised by this when I inspected my foot and the bottom edge of my robe.

I was enjoying watching Jesus as He laughed and played with the children. It seems that He never wants to stop. Around and around they would go. Oh, how Jesus loves the children! The angels also stood by and watched as God played with these little ones. "Suffer not the little ones when they come my way. For I love the little children, and now it is My turn to play," I heard Jesus say.

Grounded in the Love of God

These precious children had no cares and were content and full of life. They were fully aware of, and rooted and grounded in the perfect love of God. Somehow I was aware that many of these children that had come to heaven were previously the fetuses that had been aborted before they could live their God-ordained lives. Others were the precious children that had been lost by grieving parents. After a while these children of the Most High moved on up the meadow chasing a colorful swarm of butterflies. The butterflies they were chasing after were incredible in their colors. These butterflies seemed to actually radiate hues I have never witnessed upon the earth. They floated freely by on the gentle breezes in the meadow of Psalm 23, and the children seemed to enjoy an eternal "game" of chase with these ethereal creatures.

I watched this scenario repeat itself dozens of times that afternoon. As I lay upon my beautiful quilt, I just thought, "I wish that I could give her that butterfly to make her happy." I watched her pursue her heart's desire for another hour or so. Each time the butterfly would seemly allow her to almost capture it but at the last instant it would just fly right by her head and make its escape. Somehow, I know that she did not have any desire to harm the delicate creature. She just wanted to behold its beauty a little closer.

To my astonishment the perfect purple butterfly made its way in my direction and seemed to float down directly at me. It seemed to be coming in for a "landing," just like an airplane would upon the earth. I smiled and held out my right index finger. The delicate creature glided onto my index finger to make a perfect landing. I looked carefully at the butterfly as it flexed its translucent wings right before my eyes. As it moved its wings slowly back and forth in front of my eyes, phosphorescent colors reflected from its perfectly shaped wings sending out rays and beams of different colored glory. It was then that I realized why the little girl seemed to be so fascinated with this one special butterfly.

Butterfly Kisses

As the Lord and I lay down and rested on the blankets, the Lord was smiling at me graciously. These blankets are incredible. They are intricately sewn and made of the finest fabrics and materials. They are bright in color and are made of a patchwork of silks and other fine materials. The four friendly angels always prepare a place for us in the Psalm 23 meadow, and they always unroll these incredibly beautiful blankets for the Lord and me to rest upon. Not only are the blankets that we use for our picnics soft, but they smell like frankincense too. It is a joy when they touch my skin and when their fragrance reaches my nose! I love to lie at the feet of Jesus on those heavenly blankets. The perfect butterfly lingered upon my finger for a moment and seemed to look into my eyes. It took its proboscis and caressed the skin of my finger near my finger nail.

The thought occurred to me that the butterfly was "kissing" me. That made me think about writing a song titled "Butterfly Kisses." As this thought entered into my mind, one of the angels standing nearby moved a little closer to the Lord and me. He smiled and his perfectly formed teeth seemed to reflect the glory hovering around the Psalm 23 meadow at that instant. I was looking at the perfect butterfly kissing my finger when I saw the little girl run up from the corner of my eye. She was laughing and smiling as she ran up to me. Then she stopped and became silent for a moment. Then she sat down beside me and looked at the perfect butterfly for a tender moment. Her beautiful light blue eyes were big and I could discern the fascination that she held for this perfect butterfly. In fact, I realized that she considered this special butterfly to be her own butterfly, her pet.

As a gentle breeze ruffled her long wispy blond hair she turned slightly to look into my eyes. As she looked at me I moved my right index finger closer to her so that she could get a closer look at the special butterfly. Then the butterfly inched up my finger until it was standing on the tip of my finger flexing its amazing wings. The little girl with the beautiful blond hair slowly raised her right hand up and pointed at my finger with her delicate little index finger. Slowly she brought the tip of her finger up to gently touch the tip of my right index finger. When our fingers touched the special butterfly crawled across the bridge formed to sit upon her finger. Then the butterfly began to flutter its wings back and forth very quickly as if excited. It seemed to me that the angels nearby swooned. Then the little girl sat down on the quilt and began to inspect the special butterfly.

Awash in His Love

The butterfly began to move in a circular motion on her tiny finger and seemed to be allowing her to inspect it very closely. The little girl with the curly blond hair held the purple butterfly up into the sunshine just in front of her freckled face. After a few moments she began to giggle, and the Lord began to giggle with her. She turned and smiled at Jesus. Then Jesus looked deeply into her beautiful light blue eyes and smiled back at her as they were giggling and laughing there. The butterfly seemed to dance for them at that instant as she held out her finger for Jesus to see the perfect butterfly for Himself. I was awash in the love that was pouring out from the Lord for the little girl at that moment. Somehow I understood that she had died as a toddler upon the earth. I knew that her parents had loved her so very much, but they had faith that they would see her again in heaven. I also knew that butterflies had decorated her bedroom upon the earth.

  Slowly, she smiled and stood up, with the special butterfly still dancing on her forefinger. I watched as she slowly and deliberately raised her arm to allow the butterfly to be free to fly away. The special butterfly seemed to dance for us all for a moment longer on her little finger flexing its amazing wings. It did a pirouette and gracefully launched itself into the air on one of the gentle breezes that waft though Psalm 23. The little girl placed her hands upon her hips and giggled with renewed vigor. She stood beside us for a moment and watched the special butterfly float away on the winds of heaven.

Then she turned and smiled at Jesus and then at me and began to laugh merrily as she ran after her special friend to renew their game of chase. The angels were all looking on in amazement, as were Jesus and the other children. I did not quite understand. One of the angels spoke up saying, "She has been chasing that one special butterfly for eternity, and this day it has been given to her by your hand!" The angel that spoke seemed to be astonished. The angel smiled at me then as if to say, "Thank you," and a look of astonishment eclipsed his face. I smiled back at him then I turned to look at the Lord. Jesus was also smiling broadly and His eyes were shining with love. The little girl just let the special purple butterfly fly away freely on the winds of heaven. Then she began to chase it again, running back down the meadow with renewed enthusiasm and giggly laughter. Soon all of the other children and angels chased after her, singing and tumbling as they went. I was enamored at the goodness of God. I was in awe of Jesus and the love He carries for all of the little children. They are indeed, special to Him.

Greatest in the Kingdom

Suffer not the little children, for this is truly their land. The angels in heaven and children are singing. They are playing across the land—just as Jesus is playing and we can listen to

His sayings. Jesus calls the little children to Him, and sits in the midst of them, and says (Matthew 18:3-5):

> *Assuredly, I say to you, unless you are converted and become as little children, you will by no means enter the kingdom of heaven. Therefore whoever humbles himself as this little child is the greatest in the kingdom of heaven. Whoever receives one little child like this in My name receives Me.*

Several years later, as I read this document that had been captured from that old computer, it struck me as powerful and possibly a parabolic experience. I committed a season of prayer over this vision. I believe what I saw and experienced in Heaven was real. Jesus does in fact love the children. The Lord especially loves those who are orphans. Perhaps many of the children that I saw in Heaven in this experience had died prematurely of natural causes of accidents. However, it is also possible that most of the children that I played with in Psalm 23 were the ones that were aborted on earth. Nonetheless, God has a plan and a special place and home for them in the heavenly realm. In the next chapter we travel into the Father's vineyard to see how Jesus and God's angels are working in that amazing heavenly place.

CHAPTER 22

The Lord's Manicured Gardens

After a while the Lord stood up, and I realized that it was time for a walk. Sometimes the Lord invites me to go for long walks with Him. I love to walk with Jesus. I know that He will show me some new places and give me more revelation of the places around the Father's mansion. Jesus smiled at me and took my left hand in His as He began to lead me. This was the first time that I had looked closely and studied the scars of His hands. Jesus allowed me to place my index finger into the indention where the nail pierced His palm. He was very patient with me. Somehow I knew that many had done the same thing. I took the forefinger of my right hand and traced the outline of the wound. When I did this the reality of His sacrifice for me brought tears to my eyes. Jesus reached out with His right hand and gently wiped away my tears. This brought a smile to my face again.

Then the Lord led me back to the bank of the river of life that meanders through the grassy meadow of Psalm 23. I thought that Jesus may have wished to dive back into the depths of the water again. He did not. He said, "Come with me." It is a good idea to follow Jesus. When we reached the edge of the water Jesus simply stepped out onto the water and began to walk on the river. This was not a surprise to me because I have witnessed the Lord walk across the still waters here many times before. What surprised me was I was also walking on the waters with Him. Jesus held my left hand gently in His nail-scarred right hand and gently led me out onto the crystal clear waters of the river of life. I could feel the cool water on the soles of my bare feet. I looked up at Jesus in surprise to see a beaming smile crease His face reassuring me.

A Supernatural Walk

As we walked across the river of life I noticed that our four angelic friends were waving at us from the arched wooden bridge that spans the river in this section of the Psalm 23 meadow. They waved and smiled and I smiled back, and somehow I knew that they would be meeting the Lord and me in a little while. The bridge is beautiful yet simple. I know that it is thousands of years old, yet it is in immaculate condition. Colorful flowers meet its base on each end and there is a stone walkway that leads to and from it in this place. That walkway eventually leads up to the Father's mansion and also through the Lord's gardens. The pathway also passes by the fountain of living waters in the garden. Sometimes I stop there and an angel will give me a clean crystal goblet to drink from. The water at the fountain of living waters is always fresh, clear, and refreshing.

The Lord told me that He wanted to show me something. When we reached the other side of the river of life, He took me up to a very high mountain. When we reached the top we sat together on a large stone bench. It was about twenty-four inches high and about eighteen inches wide. The view from there was breathtaking. We could see for hundreds of miles in every direction. This is Heaven, and is beautiful beyond words. I was in awe. I sat with Jesus in silence for a long while just taking in as much of the view as I could. I was mesmerized by the beauty of this place. The mountains here were truly colossal, and I do not believe that there are any mountains this immense upon the earth. I soaked in the love and majesty of the Lord as I gazed upon the incredible view before us. I knew that this was a very special place. It is a secret place. It is the secret place of the Most High (Psalm 91:1). I took the time to examine the vista in all 360 degrees around us. Off to the south in the great distance I could make out a massive and well-manicured vineyard.

The Secret Place

I had a knowing that it was also a very special place. For some reason I had the revelation that I would return to be with Jesus in this place in the future. But I put that out of my thoughts as it seemed that the Lord had wanted for me to look at the vineyard. It was the reason for our hike to the summit of the mountain. Jesus asked me, "Would you like to see My Father's vineyard?" I immediately agreed, saying, "Yes, Lord," and asked the Lord to take me there. What you are about to read now took place over the course of several days and several visits to the Lord in the heavenly places. It never occurred to me to write these experiences down nor did I ever have any intention to do so. I had purposed to keep them treasured within my heart. I would not have written any of this had it not been for the

Lord bidding me to do so. Let me share with you the things that Jesus showed me in the vineyard during that season.

The Cares of This World

I entered my little prayer room in desperation. Recently, I had done this many times as the cares of this world had weighed heavily upon me. The frustrations of a busy work day clung to me like a spider's web, and I longed to be in the presence of the Lord. Even though I was still hot and sweaty, I knelt down and began to pray. It was just past 3 p.m. on a sunny hot afternoon. This seemed like just another time of seeking God's face. However, as I called on the name of the Lord, His presence began to envelop me washing away the cares of my day and something very special began to unfold.

As the anointing of the Holy Spirit and the love of God met me in my little prayer closet, I began to weep as something precious bubbled up from some deep and forgotten place within me. The presence of the Lord began to refresh me again. I fell prostrate on the old shag carpet. The glory of God began to wash over me in waves. Unexpectedly, I found myself under a heavy weighty blanket of glory and it felt as if warm sand had glued me to the prayer room floor. I was no longer able to move my body as the tangible presence of the Lord seemed to bond me to the carpet.

I simply luxuriated in His presence and tears flowed freely from my eyes. What a precious thing it was to feel the love of Jesus wash over me this way. I lay there in His presence for the longest time. It may have been hours; I really don't know. I was lost in God's presence when suddenly a familiar sensation began to spring up from within my body. Once again I could feel my spirit as it seemed to be launched up through the ceiling of my little prayer room.

Twinkling

When I opened my eyes I could see the little house at 121 Beech Street as it grew smaller below me. In the twilight I could see the lights of the city twinkling and growing more distant underneath me. It seemed as if my spirit was being hurled through the atmosphere and I passed supernaturally higher and higher until I could see the planet Earth far below.

As I accelerated upward brilliant phosphorescent colors blurred past me at incredible speeds. I looked to my left to see an angel smile at me. This angelic escort was holding my left hand and he was helping to orchestrate this trip into the heavenly places. However, I was not the least bit frightened because I had been in this place before. I had seen this angel before, and I knew where he was leading me to. In fact, I relaxed and enjoyed the sensation as my spirit was launched through time and space and I saw mesmerizing lights streaming past me. The feeling was wonderful and the abiding presence and love of Christ continued to wrap me in a warm blanket of His love.

My spirit continued to accelerate supernaturally through heavenly places, and the experience lasted for quite a while. I twisted, turned, and traveled through time and space as my spirit was being catapulted into heaven. After a time, I began to discern a familiar place and I came in for a "landing" much like water that spurts out from a faucet. I landed on my hands and knees.

Immediately, four angels gathered around me helping me to stand upright. They were all taller than me and radiated the love of God. They smiled at me gently as they helped me to my feet. I was a little wobbly. I looked into each angel's beautiful eyes. What lovely and caring eyes these angels have. I looked at each one in turn and each one smiled at me greeting me and making me feel totally secure, safe, and welcome in this place. I had been to this place before.

My angelic friends were all dressed in immaculate white garments. After I looked into their eyes I looked down at my feet and I noticed that I too was now robed in white garments too. My feet were bare and I stood on a beautiful stone pathway. I've seen this pathway before and I know that it leads up to the Father's house and to the place I call the great banquet hall.

Amazing Works of Art

The amazing thing about these stone walkways in this place is that each stone fits perfectly into the next and there is no mortar in the seams. In the past I've actually gotten down on my hands and knees to examine these pathways carefully. I could not find any chisel or tool marks and the stones were perfectly smooth. Each stone is perfectly and precisely joined to the next in a way that is not humanly possible. They are made of a beautiful light colored stone and are cool under the soles of your bare feet. These pathways are actually amazing works of art in themselves.

On either side of the stone pathways, which are in the Lord's manicured gardens, the grass is meticulously trimmed. In fact, it appeared to me that the grass was living as I had walked on these pathways in the past with the Lord. It seems as if the grass and the tiny flowers there would turn and follow the Son of God as He passed by. They appear to be attracted to Jesus. I found this quite amazing and went to great pains to observe how the grass and flowers turned into the direction of Jesus as He walked by. I had invested hours in the past just examining the magnificent tiny flowers in the grasses in these heavenly gardens. Even the tiniest flowers have a wonderful aroma.

As I took my eyes from my feet and looked into the faces of the four angels around me they smiled once more and waved goodbye. And I found myself alone on the pathway of God. Off to my left I saw the stone stairway that leads up to the mansion. I often ascend that stairway to be with the Lord Jesus and dine with Him in the great banquet hall. The stones of that stairway are also perfect and many beautiful flowers and vines grow near that walkway. Ahead of me and in the distance I could see the glory of God as it hovered around the mountains there. These magnificent mountain ranges are hundreds of miles away, but the air is so crystal clear here and these heavenly mountains are very easy to see even at this distance. They seemed to radiate a majestic royal purple hue in the heavenly light. Lightening periodically flashed within the dark clouds of glory that hovered around the Father's throne.

The Lord's Rose Garden

Further down to my right I saw the gardens. The Lord Jesus has taken me into those gardens before and had shown me an area where He has thousands of manicured rose bushes. On that day Jesus and I invested a whole day just looking at all the different colored roses. We would smell them and then the Lord would smile at me with great delight when He would find one that was especially pleasing to Him. During the tour of the rose garden, I was surprised at how tenderly and intimately Christ knew each plant. In fact, God loves every plant and longs for each one to bear beautiful flowers (John 15:5, 8).

The Lord's rose garden is carefully tended and manicured by angelic beings. These angels were gardeners and they were assigned to keep God's gardens manicured and in perfect shape. These angels work in the Lord's rose gardens year round because the grounds are so massive. I found it amazing that these angels were not in the least bit dirty and their robes were always perfectly white and clean. Obviously these angelic gardeners are very good at what they do. I believe that at times God sends angels like this to earth in order to help people with their crops. Perhaps that is what happened in situations like the one portrayed in the movie *Faith Like Potatoes*?

As Jesus and I were leaving the rose garden that day, I passed nearby one of these angels. At that instant it occurred to me that I was seeing a member of the great cloud of witnesses (Hebrews 12:2). This angel smiled at me and there was tenderness and a love that exuded from its presence. I had an understanding that this angel or this member of the great cloud of witnesses had once been a gardener upon the Earth. In fact, gardening was their passion in life and the work it is doing in the Lord's garden was the fulfillment of the desires of his heart (Psalm 37:4). The angel smiled at me a second time and nodded as if to confirm what I was feeling.

Your Life's Passion

As I passed by the thought occurred to me that as when I'm absent from my body (die) the Lord will allow me to pursue a passion that I loved upon the Earth (2 Corinthians 5:8). At that moment a gentle breeze blew my robe and ruffled my hair and I could smell the river which runs through the garden. As my attention was drawn to that beautiful crystal clear river, a thought came into my mind. Perhaps I could be like this gardener caring for the Lord's rose gardens. Perhaps I should oversee the river of life and invest my days fishing there in heaven. A big smile grew across my face with this thought, and I turned to see Jesus smiling at me in agreement. These memories of my past visits to the gardens of the Lord began to fade, and I found myself alone on the paths to the garden. I continued to walk and enjoy the sights, sounds, and smells of heaven along the way.

I found myself looking out across the gardens as the four angels were going their own separate ways. They had come to help me, to greet me, and to welcome me again. I took a deep breath and inhaled perfectly pure air into my lungs once again. I could smell the wonderful fragrances of the flowers that grew in abundance in that special place. I stood there for a moment taking it all in. Every single one of my five senses was on overload! It was such a pleasure to be back in the Lord's gardens, and I noticed for the first time the sound of ethereal angelic worship was lingering in the air around me. The air actually seemed to be alive in this special place, and it was endued with the power and the presence of the Lord Jesus. Even the sky radiates the presence and love of God in heaven.

God's glory is the luminescence of heaven just as God's glory is the atmosphere of heaven.

CHAPTER 23

The Lion of Judah

I smiled and began to walk along the perfectly manicured path. I had walked about one hundred yards on the path of God just examining my surroundings when I saw some movement to my left. I stopped to see what it was. For a moment my heart leapt into my throat as I saw a large male lion rise up and stretch. As this massive lion yawned, I could see its fangs; however, I did not feel threatened by this beast. Nevertheless, I was very surprised to see a lion on the loose in this place.

In fact, he seemed absolutely beautiful as he stretched out his front paws and arched his back up into the shining phosphorescent glory. The heavenly light glistened off of the lion's golden mane and for a moment it seemed to actually glow! He yawned broadly again and began to leisurely walk towards me slowly wagging his tail. I stood frozen on the stone pathway with my heart beating within my chest. I was aware of the coolness of the stones against my bare feet.

The lion continued to walk towards me looking at me eye to eye. His beautiful mane was ruffled by a gentle breeze as he stared into my eyes for a fleeting second. For a moment the thought entered my mind that I should run, but I knew I was safe and I continued to watch this magnificent creature as he deliberately covered the last few feet between us.

The lion walked right up to me. His head was level with my shoulders! He looked up at me slightly and then he licked me! He licked my face with his oversized and very wet textured tongue. Then the lion began to lick my left hand and my left arm. I was surprised to discover that the lion's saliva had the fragrance of frankincense. I was also aware that the lion's saliva contained healing properties; it was anointed! I reached out with my right hand and patted him on top of his massive head. He licked me a few more times. The lion seemed to be purring as he shot me a parting glance.

This divine lion had beautiful yellow eyes and they seemed to radiate the love of God too. I could have sworn that the lion smiled me as he walked on by and settled down nearby in the shade under what seemed to be flowering magnolia tree. I took a deep breath and laughed. Perhaps I had just met the Lion of the tribe of Judah? As I walked down the path I glanced over my shoulder to see my new friend lay back down for a nap. I continued to walk down the path pondering being licked by a lion and what that might mean. As I walked along I looked at the grass and the tiny flowers that were in it. The flowers and the grass seemed to be alive; in fact, they seem to be looking at me. So I actually got down on my hands and knees and examined them for a few minutes. I could have sworn that there were tiny voices within the grasses praising God down there.

CHAPTER 24

The Pathways of the Lord

After a while I continued to amble on the pathway of the Lord and enjoy the atmosphere of heaven. I was lost in my thoughts as I luxuriated in the majesty of this astonishing place. In my heart a desire began to spring up. The thought of walking into the gardens instead of going up into the house today came into my mind. So at the place where the paths diverged, I veered to the right and started to walk down to the gardens proper. It was wonderful to be in this place again.

The gentle breezes carried the aromas of heaven, and angelic worship rode on the winds of paradise too. At that moment I heard the roar of a lion behind me. When I turned to look at him, I saw Jesus waving at me! That really surprised me. The Lord turned and walked up the hill. So I continued down the pathway further into the manicured gardens. There had been a desire within my heart to explore this area of heaven for a long time. From time to time I would stop to smell a flower or to look at some unusual plant or feature of the gardens. There are amazing assortments of exotic plants that grow in abundance along the pathways of God in the rose gardens. I was really enjoying this afternoon in heaven, and by now all the cares of my earthly day simply vanished.

As I strolled along I came to the top of a knoll and below me I could see the place where there is an extensive maze in the garden of the Lord. I had been to this place before with Jesus but now I was alone. Yet within me there was a burning desire to go down to one of the fountains of life that is there in the center of the maze. As I entered the maze I was once again astonished at how beautiful and how immaculately maintained the plants of the maze are.

The maze consists of bushes which are perfectly healthy and which all are covered in beautiful flowers. Each section of the maze has different colored flowers and the colors seem to blend perfectly and seamlessly together from section to section. In fact, the way the colors blend together is quite striking to behold. The colors blend together in the same way that the colors of the rainbow mesh flawlessly into one another.

The flowers give off wonderful heavenly aromas as you walk from section to section. Your sense of smell is treated to many different fragrances as you pass between them just as your eyes are tickled by the multitude of various colors. As I walked through the rows of the maze, the peace and presence of Jesus was with me and the cares of the world were totally forgotten and left behind. I was lost in paradise.

Heavenly VIPs

From time to time I would see other people walking in the maze. At one point I passed a very elderly man and woman who were strolling through the garden hand in hand. It was apparent to me that they were in love. To be as old as they seemed to be they also appeared to be in remarkably good

The Pathways of the Lord

health. They talked to one another and laughed as they strolled along. As I passed by them they looked at me and greeted me with a smile. Their beautiful blue eyes twinkled in the brilliant evening sunshine.

I realized that these two people have been in God's garden for an eternity. In my heart I desired to stop them and engage them in conversation. I was very curious and would have loved to ask them a whole bunch of questions. I was certain that they knew a lot about the Lord's garden. I wanted to find out who they were. I sensed that they were quite important, heavenly VIPs. Somehow I also knew I would be interrupting their special time together. So I simply smiled back at them and passed on by quietly. That seemed like the right thing to do.

I stopped after I had walked several yards and glanced back over my shoulder. I was drawn to them for some unknown reason, perhaps it was the anointing of the Holy Spirit that seemed to diffuse from them. They continued to walk and talk in the garden. For a moment they also stopped and turned to look back at me as well. For a fleeting second I thought about running back to speak to them. They waved to me and smiled and turning they continued on their way. Somehow I understood that this couple was very special God. So, I chose to honor and respect their privacy and continued on my way too.

I understood that they had been in the Lord's garden for a very long time. Perhaps longer than anyone else save for the Trinity. I was certain of the fact that these two had a lot of revelation about this place. So I wanted to talk to them about some of the hidden mysteries I had seen here in the heavenly realms. For instance, did the grass and tiny flowers in this place really worship God with their voices? The elderly couple, the heavenly VIPs, carried themselves with a sense of nobility, yet they also seemed to be very humble and meek. These two were truly friends of God. Somehow I had the revelation that the Lord had walked with them in the garden in the cool of the day many times before.

I began to wonder what things they had talked about with God. It would have been quite interesting to know, but somehow I also understood that the timing for this was not quite right. But I also had a knowing that I would have an opportunity to speak to this amazing couple at my leisure in the future. After I waved to them I dropped my right hand back down to my side. As I did it brushed against the material of my white robe and it seemed smoother than fine silk. I wondered just exactly what kind of material it was fashioned from. I had so many questions about this place. I suppose that it would take an eternity to have them all answered. I continued walking through the maze of the Lord's rose garden lost in my thoughts and meandering on the pathways of God.

CHAPTER 25

The Water of Life

I walked through the garden for what seemed like hours. The same presence and the same glory and love of God that had rested upon me in my prayer room were still lingering upon me now as I walked in the garden in the cool of the day. As I made my way through the maze, I knew my destination was the fountain of living waters. I had been to that special place before. In fact, Jesus had taken me to this particular fountain one of the first times I had come to be with Him in these heavenly places during this special season. There are many fountains like this one in the realms of heaven.

On the day I am speaking of, the Lord and I had left the great banquet hall and we had walked down the stone stairway from the back of the great banquet hall together. That winding stone stairway leads down to the stone pathways which I was walking upon now. Those pathways meander freely through the Lord's gardens and eventually they lead to the fountain of living water. It is a very nice walk, quite refreshing, you see; and I hope that you can enjoy it sometime too. When the Lord and I had come to this fountain of living waters that day there were many people who were fellowshipping around the fountain. And they all seemed very glad that Jesus had come to be with them.

Crystal Clear Waters

The Lord and I walked over and sat down on the edge of the fountain because it makes a good bench. In fact, I think that it was designed that way, as a place for folks to just rest and refresh themselves. The fountain is amazing. The fountain of living waters is about sixty feet or more in diameter and the top of the fountain is about forty-five feet high. In fact it is quite large. This one is set in the center of the gardens and is a real focal point of this region of the heavenly realms. I guess that is why it is positioned in the center of the Lord's manicured gardens.

Many people come to drink of the crystal clear waters that flow from the top of the fountain. The Lord showed me that the waters come from the river of God. I understand that the river of God is the same river that flows from the very throne room of the Father. This is described very well in Revelation, chapter 22. I believe the first two verses of that chapter are all about the river of God I had seen, swam in, and tasted:

> *And he showed me a pure river of water of life, clear as crystal, proceeding from the throne of God and of the Lamb. In the middle of its street, and on either side of the river, was the tree of life, which bore twelve fruits, each tree yielding its fruit every month. The leaves of the tree were for the healing of the nations.*

In fact, the river of God is also the same river that flows through the meadow of Psalm 23. That is the place where those healing trees are flourishing and always in bloom. These healing trees remind me of the majestic magnolia trees on earth, but the flowers of the heavenly trees have much larger blooms and flowers. Those blooms permeate the air in the meadow of Psalm 23 with an exquisite aroma that is just delicious; in fact you can actually taste the fragrance! I will describe that in more detail later, but the fountain of life is just exquisite!

The fountains are made of beautiful white stones, and just like the pathways in the garden there seems to be no mortar or tool marks from the fountain's construction. The white stones are immaculate and the water within the fountain is crystal clear. In fact it seems to be alive.

In the center of the fountain of living water is a tower, and from the top of that place the crystal clear water bubbles out. It bubbles out like an artesian well, but I am sure that its source is the river of God. It flows down from the top from intricately carved basins to the larger pool where Jesus and I were seated on the wide ledge. The holy water flows majestically down from an intricately carved basin to the next intricately carved basin below.

This ledge is the perfect size to sit upon and relax and be refreshed by the living water. It is about twenty-four inches wide and is also made of the same immaculate white stone. As the water tumbles down it makes delightful sounds that mingle with the ethereal sounds of harps, flutes, and various other stringed instruments. The sound at the fountain of living waters is extremely peaceful as angelic singing and worship mingles with the sounds of the falling waters of life. Here even the fountains of living water seem to worship the Messiah.

On the day which I am speaking of, I was sitting beside the fountain of living waters with Jesus. The Lord made a motion with His right hand signaling for an angel who was nearby to come over to us. The angel carried a serving tray made of the finest materials and he handed to the Lord a beautiful crystal clear goblet. Jesus took the goblet and with His left hand He held it out so that the living water from the fountain of life trickled into it from one of the intricately carved lower basins filling the crystal clear goblet with the crystal clear water of life. When it was full Jesus extended the goblet to me. The water is perfectly pure and holy.

The Unfathomable Love of God

With His left hand the Lord handed me the goblet with the crystal clear pure water. As Jesus stretched forth His hand, I could see the place where the nails had pierced His body and for a moment tears filled my eyes, and a deep sense of sadness welled up from within my spirit again. At that instant it seemed as if it grew very silent near the fountain of living water and I was aware of the fact that the people and angels nearby were looking at us. More precisely they were looking at me with great sympathy.

Sadness is not very common in heaven. I reached out with my right hand and took the crystal goblet from the Messiah in this silence. When I did my fingertips touched His hand and the sadness that I had felt instantly disappeared. With my left hand I quickly wiped away a tear which had escaped from my left eye. As I looked up I saw the Messiah smiling lovingly at me. His beautiful eyes contained the unfathomable everlasting love which God has for you and me.

The Water of Life

When I took the goblet into my hands, I saw that very ornate designs have been carefully etched into the crystal. I studied the intricacy of the fine design in amazement for a moment. Its detail was bewildering to me as I had never seen such craftsmanship upon the earth. When I glanced up I saw the angel hand the Lord Jesus Christ a second goblet and once again Jesus filled the glass with living water from the fountain of life. Once again waves of God's love washed over me. As I sat on the edge of the fountain in the presence of Jesus, I was aware of the enormity of the great sacrifice that He had made for me and for all of mankind.

The love of God that the Messiah has for every tongue, every tribe, and every nation is impossible for us to understand with our carnal minds and human intellect. At that moment Jesus raised His glass indicating that we should drink. I raised the crystal goblet to my lips and began to drink the water of life. It felt as if a supernatural cleansing and inner healing was taking place within my soul. As the water passed over my lips and down my esophagus and into my stomach, the power of God washed over me. I looked up to see the Messiah drinking the crystal clear water from the fountain of life too. When He finished the Lord handed His crystal goblet to the angel standing nearby and smiled at me.

I was aware of the fact that I could also hand my glass to the angel, but instead I had a very overwhelming desire to drink deeply from the water of life. So, I held the crystal goblet back out to the same place Jesus had, where the living water was flowing freely from the fountain of life. I filled my goblet again, and once again I drank freely from the living water. I did this several times, as the Lord watched me drinking heartily again and again. He smiled at me like a proud papa on his child's birthday.

Jesus' smile indicated that He was overjoyed that I was drinking more from the fountain of life! However, He surprised me when He began laughing heartily. And at that moment I realized that I could have as much of this precious water as I desired at any time I was thirsty. I began to laugh too, and we sat together on the side of the fountain of life laughing together wholeheartedly for a long time. Soon everyone in the area was also laughing cheerfully, and the love of God enveloped me in a fresh way as I saw how the Lord was laughing and enjoying Himself by the fountain of living water. After a few minutes the Lord looked lovingly and intently into my eyes.

The Lord held out a new crystal clear goblet which was filled with the water of life. The Messiah held it in His mighty right hand as He spoke. For a moment there was a great silence and then Jesus spoke emphatically to me. But I understood that what He was saying was for anyone who was thirsty for more of God.
The Lord Jesus said this:

> If anyone thirsts, let him come to Me and drink. Let them come to me all you who are thirsty. I will pour water on him who is thirsty. Let everyone know who thirsts, Come to the waters; and you who have no money, Come, buy and eat. Yes, come, buy wine and milk without money and without price. For there is a fountain and whoever drinks of the water that I shall give him will

The Water of Life

never thirst. But the water that I shall give him will become in him a fountain of water springing up into everlasting life. He who believes in Me, as the scripture has said, out of his heart will flow rivers of living water. If anyone thirsts, let him come to Me and drink. It is done! I am the Alpha and the Omega, the Beginning and the End. I will give of the fountain of the water of life freely to him who thirsts. He who overcomes shall inherit all things, and I will be his God and he shall be My son. Come! And let him who hears say, "Come!" And let him who thirsts come. Whoever desires let him take the water of life freely. He who drinks this water out of his heart will flow rivers of living water.

When Jesus had finished speaking it was as if a crescendo of angelic worship seemed to instantaneously explode in the air surrounding the Messiah, and the glory of God multiplied around us again. Jesus continued to smile lovingly at me and gazed intently into my eyes for several precious moments. We continued to sit at the fountain for a while and I drank even more of the living waters. Then we arose and walked down into the meadow of Psalm 23. Several angels accompanied us on that day, and I remember the wonderful time that we had as we broke bread together on a blanket there by the river of God.

CHAPTER 26

The Fountain of Living Waters

As I was walking down the pathway remembering that encounter at the fountain of living waters, a smile spread across my face. I recalled that experience with fondness and assurance and I was glad that I was walking on the path of God to return to the fountain of life. Within my spirit a desire grew to sit on the ledge of the fountain of life and to drink from a new crystal goblet from the waters of life. After all they flow freely from the very throne of the Father and of the Lamb, and I could have as much as I liked. And this day I was very hot and very thirsty.

A little while later I came to the spot where Jesus and I had previously drunk freely from the fountain of life. There were several people and angels milling around in the area adjacent to the fountain of life. I sat down by myself in the exact spot where Jesus had spoken to me by the fountain of life. I closed my eyes for a few minutes and pondered these things in my heart. I realized that I had been walking for quite a while, and I had covered a long distance on this visit. It occurred to me that I was very thirsty, and as this thought passed through my mind someone tapped me lightly on my left shoulder breaking my concentration.

I turned and looking to my left and I recognized the same angel that had served Jesus and me. The angel that served was standing beside me with a big bright smile upon his face. In his hands was the same serving tray and upon it were two crystal goblets. Suddenly the winds began to swirl around us ever so gently and I felt the presence of the Lord increase. I saw the angelic being look behind me with his piercing blue eyes. As I turned to see what he was looking at, I saw the Lord walking up to the fountain of life. I fell down upon my knees and grasped His feet. I saw the scars of the nails.

Once again I began to weep. The Lord placed His right hand upon my head and I stood to my feet. Jesus motioned for me to sit down beside Him on the ledge of the fountain of life. Once again a tear began to roll slowly down my left cheek. The Lord sat down beside me smiling at me. Jesus smiled at me again, and noticing my tears He reached out with His right hand and He wiped away my tears (Isaiah 25:8). When the Messiah touched my tears, I smiled too. At that moment the angel handed Jesus a crystal clear goblet and the Lord reached out with His left hand and filled it with the living water from the fountain of life. Then He handed it to me.

Waves of glory and love washed over me and the peace of God which passes our ability to comprehend filled my entire being. The angel offered a second crystal clear goblet to the Lord and He also filled that one. I could feel the intricate designs that were etched into the fine crystal under my fingertips. The Lord raised his glass and we drank freely of the living water together once again. The power of God coursed through my being and I felt the healing power of the Lord refreshing me. It seemed as if my ability to taste, touch, hear, smell and

The Fountain of Living Waters

feel were suddenly supernaturally multiplied. And the love of God began to well up from within my heart.

I tarried with Christ for a long time at the fountain of living waters. He spoke many things into my heart that day. After a time I knew that it was time for me to return home. I stood up beside Jesus and He looked deeply and lovingly into my eyes. He said, "You are always welcome here." Looking deeply into my eyes the Lord told me to go now and write down all of the things that I had both seen and heard when I returned to my little house at 121 Beech Street (Acts 4:20).

With that the Lord said goodbye and turned to walk away down one of the paths that leads through His gardens. I sat back down on the ledge of the fountain of living waters and watched the Lord as He retreated in the garden. I saw a small child run to Jesus and the Lord swept him up in His arms. They laughed and played for several minutes until the boy ran back to join a lot of other children who were also playing a game in the gardens nearby. Angels were watching over the children and attending to their every need as they laughed and played innocently in this delightful and supernatural paradise.

I stayed upon the ledge of the fountain of living waters for a long time pondering these things in my heart. Who was that elderly couple? Who did all of those children belong to, and why were they here? Why don't more of God's people come and drink freely from the fountain of living waters? I turned to splash some of the living water into my face. In an instant I found myself hurtling back through time and space. I could see the planets whizzing past again. I saw my angelic escort by my side once more. I could see the earth below and finally I saw the little house at 121 Beech Street. In the instant that the living waters touched my face I was sucked back into my body and I arose from the shag carpet. It was now dark and I was covered with sweat. I could still smell the fragrances of the Lord's garden, and the taste of the living water still lingered in my mouth. I could still hear the crescendo of angelic worship as it swirled around me at that moment.

When I looked at the clock I was astonished to see that it was now well past 1 a.m. I had been in my tiny prayer closet nearly ten hours. Or was I? I rose up to my knees and found that it was still very difficult to move my body. When I got up to splash water on my face, I discovered gold specks there. I laughed, and took a quick shower. I sat down at the keyboard of the old computer and started to write. The keyboard was also covered with golden glory dust too. As the sun began to rise, I lay down upon my bed. Later I woke up dreaming about a lion licking my face and began to laugh all over again. I woke up smiling.

CHAPTER 27

The Father's Vineyard

Jesus and I seemed to mount up as if on eagle's wings. In the next instant it seemed as if I was soaring into the heights of the heavens. I saw the mountains far below and in the far distance I could see the crystal cathedral of God. Emanating from the throne were brilliant lights and the sounds of worship such as I have never experienced. The crystal cathedral is also the source of the river of life. I saw it flow freely from the Father's throne through the heavens finally feeding the rivers that led into the great and massive vineyard. From this great height the Lord allowed me to see the true vine.

The Lord took me up into the heights of heaven and showed me the vineyard from a great distance. Then He began to take me there into the Father's vineyard on sequential visits to the heavenly realms. Jesus led me as we explored the vast vineyard on these excursions. These trips into the vineyard took place over several weeks. The Lord often led me into the Father's vineyard and we took many trips into the valley of the vineyard. We invested many days moving across the vast and massive chateau. The Father's vineyard covers hundreds of square miles. It is immense. The river of life flows and meanders through the middle of the ground and the center of the fields there. The plots of land that are in the vineyard are too numerous to number. It was from a great height that Jesus showed me the base of the great vine. The true vine is immense, and its circumference must be larger than the New Orleans Superdome, which, by the way, is the home of the Saints. The beginning of the true vine must be at least ten times the size of a superdome. It is unimaginable and I have a difficult time describing its size. What an awesome God!

Somehow I had the revelation that even though the Father's vineyard is hundreds and hundreds of square miles, each individual vine is a branch of the one true vine. Over the course of several weeks the Lord taught me in great detail that it is all one living vine. It is all one church. The vineyard is all His church and His Bride. It was only after Jesus was absolutely certain that I completely understood this fact that He actually took me to the vineyard.

The first time that I actually stepped into the vineyard I was astounded at the enormity of it all. The Lord Jesus guided me into this incredible massive living entity. We were always accompanied by four angelic beings. There were also many angels who worked in the Father's vineyard too. As we walked mile after mile, the Lord would take the time to stop and point out different places and aspects of the true vine to me. Each time He would ask me what I saw. Each time I would relate to the Lord what I was seeing. I sought to tell the Lord and relate the things that I saw in as much detail as I could. Jesus was training me. I am certain that the lessons that Jesus taught the disciples as recorded in John 15 were in much greater detail than what is actually recorded in that Gospel. Of course, this is only my opinion. It is apparent that Jesus knows every square inch of the vineyard and the true vine intimately.

That is exactly what the Holy Spirit is calling His church to today, a place of intimacy and communion with Jesus. It makes total sense that Jesus would seek a very close and personal relationship with His church and His people before His return. Jesus is calling the church into a place of friendship and intimacy. He has always desired intimacy with His children. Jesus wants to know His Bride personally! The Lord desires to have a very personal and intimate relationship with you as an individual too. We should find this very comforting.

As we walked mile by mile, the Lord would point out certain branches of the true vine. One branch the Lord showed me was very clean and orderly. This part of the vineyard even had a nice white picket fence around its boundaries. It was a very large section of the vine and the grounds around it were very well manicured and maintained. There were no weeds or tares in the rich soil near the vine. The ground had been tilled and manicured. This branch of the vineyard had many beautiful leaves upon it and they seemed to be quite healthy and in abundance.

I assumed that Jesus was very pleased with this vine. It looked very good, and it appeared to be very healthy. Then Jesus instructed me to take a closer look. I still liked the way this branch of the vine looked, and it seemed to be very healthy and vigorous. I was surprised when Jesus said, "This branch is due to be pruned by my Father soon." When the Lord said this I noticed a group of angels who were nearby. They were working on the vine pruning branches and bundling the woody materials in sheaves of sorts. I did not understand this statement because the branch looked so healthy (John 15:1-2).

Then I saw the Lord as He used His hand to reveal that though it had many leaves, this branch did not have very much fruit. The grapes were small and some were deformed. They had not developed correctly, and this was very unusual in the Father's vineyard. Jesus had to search carefully under many leaves to find these small unhealthy grapes. This particular vine was planted by the great river of living waters. Its leaves turned toward the sun and it was well groomed. In fact, it was very orderly. Yet, it did not bear good fruit. There were a few nice grapes on this section of the true vine. There were some very nice grapes even, and some choice grapes. However, it seemed that most were not fit for the harvest. Somehow I understood that the Lord only allowed grapes without spot or blemish to be harvested from the Father's vineyard. This also surprised me a little, but at the same time this fact also makes perfect sense in the Kingdom of Heaven. (See Ephesians 1:4; 5:25-27.)

Over time the Lord took great care to show me many branches of the true vine. Some looked quite undone. They had weeds and tares in the ground around the base of the vine. The fence and trellis around some of these were broken down and in disrepair. This also surprised me as well. The leaves upon these branches were not very attractive or pretty to look upon. Then the Lord took His right hand and carefully moving a set of these imperfect leaves He showed me a very large cluster of grapes from this section of the vine. What fruit! This cluster of grapes were large, juicy looking, and very beautiful. They seemed to glow in the evening sunshine, and I could see the reflection of Jesus on the skin of these grapes.

This branch of the vine had much more fruit upon it than I would have imagined. It was as if it had done exceedingly, abundantly above anything that I could have imagined. You would expect this smaller and anemic looking vine would not produce as much as the perfectly healthy and immaculate looking section of the vine. But the fruit this vine was bearing was nothing short of a miracle. I thought, "This is the anointing and grace of the Holy Spirit at work." When this thought crossed into my mind the Lord smiled at me and nodded in agreement.

Jesus rose up from His knees and we continued to walk through the Father's vineyard for hours and hours. In fact, over the next several months I was allowed to return to the heavenly realms to visit the Lord Jesus many times. On each of these successive days we returned to the Father's vineyard. After the third day of visiting the true vine, it occurred to me that Jesus was seeking to show me something very important. When this thought came into my mind the Lord spoke to me and said, "It is important that you write down the things that you see here in this place." That is the reason that I have recorded these observations from these walks throughout the Father's vineyard.

Over this season the Lord showed me many branches, and we stopped to look at these in great detail. Often we invested a lot of time with these individual sections of the true vine, and the Lord seemed to be inspecting every minute detail of these vines. Some of the branches were in great disrepair and in a poor condition. However, that did not hinder the Lord from tenderly and lovingly caring for each one. At times I heard the Lord actually pray for a section of the true vine. Several times I noticed that angels would come and care for those areas of the vines immediately after Jesus moved on. Perhaps that is why some of the branches which were in bad condition remained fruitful. In fact some of the shabbiest sections of the vine bore much fruit. Some vines in an unattended looking condition had little or no fruit, but others in a similar condition had an unbelievable bounty of fruit.

Other sections of the vine which appeared to have greater care given to the soil and which appeared to be well attended to seemed to have all leaves and very little or no fruit. Even some of the larger and healthy branches which grew very close to the river of life and which seemed to be well maintained had little or no fruit. This was a great surprise to me. In fact, I saw only a few of the large healthy looking branches which grew very near to the water of life which actually had an abundance of fruit. I was amazed that some of the vines that were much further from the source of water and which seemed to have very small branches and very few leaves also had great amounts of fruit. As time progressed I became certain that the Father's vineyard was a parabolic image of the Body of Christ and the church upon the earth.

One section of the true vine in particular stood out to me as Jesus and I inspected it. It was a very puny and scrawny looking branch. And this section of the vine was a great distance from the river of life. All of the branches around it were in a very poor condition. In fact, it appeared to me that some of those branches of the vine were about to die. This also surprised me. These branches had just a little withered fruit still remaining upon them. But not the branch that Jesus was showing me. This particular branch did not have a great deal of fruit because it was very small. However, the grapes that it was bearing were among some of the biggest and most beautiful grapes that Jesus had shown me in our extensive tour of the Father's vineyard.

When Jesus himself pointed this branch of the vine out to me I was very surprised. I noticed that there was a small spring of water nearby. Perhaps this pool was similar to an artesian well upon the Earth. It was bubbling up from the dry ground near the base of this amazing branch of the true vine. Somehow I understood that this phenomenon, where water bubbled up into the midst of a dry and thirsty land was very scriptural. And I made a mental note to search my old King James Bible when I returned back home after this trip. Later I found these scriptures in the Book of Isaiah with the help of the Holy Spirit:

Isaiah 35:5-7

> *Then the eyes of the blind shall be opened, And the ears of the deaf shall be unstopped. Then the lame shall leap like a deer, And the tongue of the dumb sing. For waters shall burst forth in the wilderness, and streams in the desert. The parched ground shall become a pool, and the thirsty land springs of water; In the habitation of jackals, where each lay, There shall be grass with reeds and rushes.*

Isaiah 55:1-2:

Ho! Everyone who thirsts, Come to the waters; And you who have no money, Come, buy and eat. Yes, come, buy wine and milk Without money and without price. Why do you spend money for what is not bread, And your wages for what does not satisfy? Listen carefully to Me, and eat what is good, And let your soul delight itself in abundance.

CHAPTER 28

Heavenly Parables and an Answered Prayer

At this point I became aware of the fact that as Jesus had been giving me a tour of the Father's vineyard over the last few weeks. It seemed clear to me that the Lord was seeking to teach me important lessons. And when I discovered those scriptures from Isaiah 35, I was certain that they perfectly represented and confirmed what I had seen with Jesus earlier in the day. These scriptures also gave me great hope because I was living in such a dry and thirsty land (Psalm 63:1). As I prayed about this, I became aware of the fact that the Lord was showing me things in a parabolic nature. Of course, Jesus often taught and spoke in parables while He walked upon the Earth. And when I realized this fact, it made perfect sense to me that the Lord would continue to use parabolic illustrations in the heavenly places. This fact gave me great peace and assurance of the things I was experiencing in the heavenly realms. Though, at times the Lord spoke very clearly to me during our times together in the heavenly places, as a man does to a friend.

As I continued to ascend into heavenly places during this extended season, the Lord Jesus continued to walk with me through the Father's vineyard. He continued to show me many different branches. We looked at all different types of branches that were connected to the one true vine. However, it seemed to me that Jesus was most pleased with the vines that did not seem to be in a likely place to flourish. Time after time when the Lord discovered beautiful fruit growing upon scrawny or unhealthy sections of the one true vine, Jesus would break out into a broad smile. And I could actually feel the pleasure that the Lord took from these unlikely places. The Lord was well pleased and has great love and compassion for the branches that had only a cluster or two of fruit. In fact, it seemed that He took great pleasure from sections of the vine like these more so than from the other larger and healthier looking branches which had mostly leaves.

Follow Jesus

When we left the branch with the artesian spring, Jesus asked me to follow Him again. I always love to follow Jesus in the heavenly realms because I know that He is about to reveal hidden secrets or mysteries to me. And this is always very rewarding. We walked together for quite a way. It seemed to me that Jesus was very focused as we were walking through that part of the Father's vineyards. I continued to study the branches and the amount of fruit on each one as the Lord Jesus had taught me to do. It was amazing because of all of the different types of branches that were to be found in this remarkable part of heaven. We were walking steadily up an incline in a section of the Father's vineyard that was cultivated upon higher elevations.

We continued to walk purposefully and after a while we came to a very small branch of the true vine. Jesus immediately knelt down beside it and began to inspect it very closely. The main branch was very small and gnarled. It appeared to be very old. There were not very many leaves upon this small branch. However, the soil around the base of the vine was tilled and well kept. There were just a few tares and weeds in this small spick-and-span part of the vineyard. This small vine had just a few clusters of grapes but they were all very nice. The grapes on this vine were not the best, but they were very good looking grapes.

Jesus pulled back the leaves and showed me a small cluster of three perfectly formed grapes. They were golden in color and there seemed to be an anointing of the Holy Spirit that emanated from the largest grape. I could tell that Jesus was very familiar with this grape personally. I was amazed that the Lord knew this one individual grape so well. There were millions and millions of grapes in the Father's vineyard. Yet, Jesus had walked miles to inspect this single grape on this day. It was as if He was being drawn to this particular grape for some unknown reason. What Jesus did next surprised me.

He reached out with His right hand and plucked this very special grape from the one true vine and looked at the grape. Suddenly I went into a vision. I saw a little grey haired widow and she was in her humble kitchen. She was kneeling beside her kitchen table with her elbows upon the little wooden chair there. She was in prayer, and she was speaking directly to Jesus. I was surprised that I could hear her prayers as I knelt beside Jesus. She was blessing her morsel of lunch.

The Power of Pure Prayer

The Lord told me to listen carefully to her as she prayed. This was the first time He had ever done this before. I was amazed that I could hear her perfectly as she prayed. It was as if the Lord allowed me to hear what He could hear. Immediately I could feel the emotions and the heartache that she was experiencing. I understood the urgency and the spirit of her prayer. It was very pure. Her prayer was very humble. Somehow I knew everything about her as she prayed to Jesus. Perhaps as I knelt so close to Jesus He allowed me to have His revelation concerning this woman's prayers and needs. Her name was Francis, but her friends and late husband Earl had called her Fannie May before they had died. She was weeping as she prayed. I was overcome with her heartfelt prayer and gut wrenching emotions that she was experiencing at that instant. Her prayer touched my spirit deeply and an unknown compassion welled up from someplace deep within me.

She was praying for her only son. Fannie May had not heard from him for years. She felt that she too was approaching the end of her days. Fannie called out in the name of Jesus. Perhaps that is what had drawn the Lord to this place today. She prayed, "O Jesus, I do not know where Timmy is. I do not know what he is about, but you do, Jesus. O God, please forgive me if I have done something to hurt him. If I have pushed Timmy away, O Lord, I repent." I knew that she had been praying this prayer for a long time, and she had touched Jesus by her heartfelt words. She had brought the Lord close to her with the purity of her heart and her repentance as she earnestly called out to the Lord this day.

Heavenly Parables and an Answered Prayer

As this vision continued the Lord looked at me and asked me what I would do. At this point it was as if we were instantly catapulted through time and space. Jesus and I were instantly in the little kitchen with Fannie May. She was upon her knees in prayer. The four angels that usually accompany me and the Lord were also in the small kitchen. Perhaps she saw the Lord's angels too. She was overcome and it seemed that she was filled with the Holy Spirit because she began to pray loudly and more intently.

Once again the Lord repeated His question to me: "What would you do?" Without thinking I instantly said, "Lord, touch the heart of her son so that he would call his mother after all of these years." Instantly it seemed as if I was traveling through time and space again and I found myself at a construction site. I recognized Timmy immediately because he had the gentle blue eyes of his mother. He was a carpenter and he was working very hard. Jesus stepped up beside him and spoke to Timmy. He stopped hammering and set his sixteen pound framing hammer down looking around for a moment. Jesus said: "You should call your mother. Tell her that you love her. Tell her that you are going to come home to see her." It appeared that the Spirit of the Lord fell upon the young man and Timmy began to weep as something broke deep down within his soul had been healed instantly in that moment.

He left work immediately to find a phone. Suddenly we were back in the kitchen with Fannie May. She was still praying when the phone rang. She got up quickly from her knees and answered it. She knew in her spirit before she picked up the phone that it was her son who was calling. Her son repented and they spoke for a long time and started the process of healing in their relationship. Timmy told Fannie May that he was going to come home. In fact, he told her that he would be there the next day. Tears of joy were streaming from her eyes, and she turned and seemed to look at Jesus one last time. Fannie May smiled at the Lord and He smiled back at her.

Instantaneously Jesus and I were back in the Father's vineyard. The Lord was still holding the perfectly formed grape in His right hand. I looked into the eyes of the Lord and saw great compassion in His eyes. Then Jesus did something amazing. He took the grape and reattached it to the one true vine. This seemed to give Him great pleasure and a smile beamed across His face. It was then that I also realized that I was crying, although I was not sad. In fact, I was elated. The Lord and I stood up and began to walk back through the Father's vineyard together. Neither one of us spoke for a long while. However, I was astonished at what I had just witnessed. I began to discern in a greater measure, and I understood that the anointing of the Holy Spirit seemed to be emanating in various degrees from many of the individual grapes that grew upon the various vines that we passed. In my mind I pondered the question of why Jesus was drawn to that place and vine that we had just visited today.

Jesus turned and smiled at me valiantly and then said, quoting Jeremiah 29:11-14:

> *For I know the thoughts that I think toward you, says the LORD, thoughts of peace and not of evil, I desire to give you a future and a hope. When you will call upon Me and*

Heavenly Parables and an Answered Prayer

> *go and pray to Me, and I will listen to you. And when my people seek Me find Me, when you search for Me with all your heart. I will be found by you....*

I remembered that Jesus had spoken those very same words over me during the first visitation of Jesus I had experienced in Springdale, Newfoundland, Canada, on November 25, 2001.

As I looked into the eyes of Jesus, revelation began to flow into my spirit about God's heart to answer all of our prayers. The Lord knows what we have need of before we even ask; but sometimes when we search for Him, He waits until the perfect time to respond. Today was the perfect time for Jesus to answer Fannie May's prayer. It was a great privilege and honor to witness such a supernatural event! In fact it was astonishing to see a prayer answered. God is listening and He will answer your prayers too.

CHAPTER 29

The Throne Room

Let me share one final depiction of heaven with you. On one occasion I had been taken up into the heavenly realms to join Jesus in the great banquet hall. After we had concluded our meal and fellowship time together, the Lord arose from the table. He smiled at me then the Lord said, "I want you to come with me today. There is something important that I want to show you."

Jesus walked along the eastern wall of the great banquet hall, and I walked in sync with Him. There was an excitement in my heart about what the Lord was about to reveal to me. By now I had been visiting the Lord for months in the heavenly realms. In my humanness I had thought that I had "seen it all." How silly was that idea? The Lord led me to a wonderfully ornate door. It was baroque looking and was covered with ornate and lavish designs. It appeared to be covered in pure gold. The heavenly light that was filtering down from the windows above seemed to create an ethereal glow within the very material of the double doors. For a moment I had wondered why I had not noticed these marvelous doors before. Then I remembered that the hidden mysteries of heaven need to be revealed to you by God.

Two of the four angels that were walking with Jesus moved forward to open this pair of ornate ancient doors as we approached. When the angels opened the doors the sound of worship exploded into the great banquet hall. Jesus entered into a magnificent hallway that led upward at a slight angle. When I stepped into the hallway, my eyes were momentarily blinded by the glory and power of the brilliant light that was emanating from the other end of the corridor. Looking down at my bare feet I saw that I was walking on a golden pathway, and this helped to magnify the luminescence of the brilliant light that was flooding into this hidden passageway. I could feel the coolness of the material of the floor, and I could also feel the tangible glory of God flowing past me in waves and billows. The glory of God blew past me like the winds of heaven. The heavy, weighty, tangible glory of God poured past me like a mighty rushing wind in this place. It was wonderful, and I could have just camped out there.

Brilliant Glory

Tears began to stream from my eyes as the weighty glory of God filled my spirit. Jesus reached out with His right arm and put His hand upon my shoulder drawing me closer to Himself, and we continued to walk together. As we reached the end of the very long corridor, the Lord stopped and turned to look deeply into my eyes. The fragrances of frankincense and myrrh that I had been experiencing over the last few months were powerful and seemed to permeate the air that was rushing over us from the room that was just a few yards ahead. As Jesus gazed into my eyes, the brilliant glory from the massive room seemed to

The Throne Room

twinkle and shimmer from His beautiful pupils. Jesus smiled at me with delight. He said, "You are always welcome in this place. Come with me now." My heart leaped with joy at these words, and I wondered where the Lord was taking me today.

With that He turned and purposely moved forward stepping through an opening into the room. I was immediately awed by the volume of the sounds in this place. I looked out to see millions and millions of people worshiping God. The sounds of worship permeated the air, and it was obvious that thousands of angels were singing in unison with the millions of people that I was seeing. In fact, there were millions of angels in this place too. I was reminded of how I had first heard angelic singers in Newfoundland back in 2001. (This incident is depicted in *Visitations of Angels and Other Supernatural Experiences #1 & #2*.) This thought made me smile. I was actually flabbergasted by the sight that lay before me. Jesus continued to walk deliberately towards the center of this massive room. On either side of us were people who were all dressed in immaculate white robes. The Lord and I were walking down a wide row that appeared to be fashioned of a golden crystalline substance. The four angels who always accompanied me in the heavenly realms were walking in step with us as we approached the center of the room.

Most of the saints in the room were so involved and engrossed in worship that they did not notice Jesus as He walked by. Occasionally, a person would see the Lord and would fall upon their face and worship the Lamb of God as He passed by. The people and angelic hosts here were singing incredibly beautiful and harmonious praises to God. The sound was the most beautiful sound that I have ever heard. They were worshiping the Lamb of God and singing songs of glory and honor to Jesus, "Holy, Holy, Holy!" There was such a powerful presence of unity, peace, and all-consuming love in this enormous place that it was simply overwhelming. I was totally enamored by what I was seeing, feeling, hearing, and experiencing.

Worthy Is the Lamb

We had begun to journey into the room from the very outer edge. I was astonished and in my mind I tried to calculate the number of individuals that were in this glorious place. It dawned upon me how the Apostle John must have felt when he said in Revelation 5:11-12:

> *I looked, and I heard the voice of many angels around the throne, the living creatures, and the elders; and the number of them was ten thousand times ten thousand, and thousands of thousands, saying with a loud voice: "Worthy is the Lamb who was slain To receive power and riches and wisdom, And strength and honor and glory and blessing!"*

The Lord continued to move steadily through the massive group of people. From the top of the path that we were on I began to understand that we were in an enormous room full of glory and ethereal light. Looking to the center I saw the source of the light. It was the throne of God. It appeared to be about a mile or more away from us now. However, I could see incredible lights and colors phosphorescing within and around the throne. These colors seemed to be living. However,

The Throne Room

the glory around the throne was also very dark at times. The Father's throne appeared to be covered in dense luminescent clouds, and every so often lightning and thunder would rumble forth from the midst of the glory making me wince. After a few claps of thunder and several flashes of lightening I became more comfortable with the mighty noises and flashing lights that were being emitted from the area of the throne. Though, it was impossible to see the image of the Father behind the dark clouds hovering around His throne. This spectacle was still quite unnerving. The reverential fear of the Lord was upon me and I fell upon my face. I was quite undone to be in this place and the reverential fear pressed in upon me all the more. Had I not been in the company of Jesus, I am not sure that I would have survived!

It became obvious to me that Jesus was headed to the throne. This understanding gave me pause and the awe of God poured over me like a river of power. The closer that we came to the throne the greater the reverential fear of the Lord grew within my spirit. As we proceeded to the throne, I purposed in my heart to study my surroundings carefully. It is actually impossible for me to accurately depict the vastness and scale of the room that the Lord and I were walking through at that moment. It is possible that the throne room was miles in circumference. However, I am certain that the room was somewhat circular with the Father's throne located perfectly in the center. This is total speculation on my behalf. The Father's throne was the source of extreme glory and power. It is possible that the Father's throne is the source of all of the light and glory in the heavenly places that I have described to you. Again, I am not certain.

There appeared to be a crystal cathedral type ceiling soaring high above the room. Around the throne in the distance was a beautiful lake or sea of crystal that appeared to flow from and have its source coming from the very throne of God. Both of these continuously reflected the lightning and glory that emanated from the Father's throne. As Jesus and I continued to walk down the sloping walkway that led to the center of the room I continued to examine my surroundings. It appeared that there were literally millions upon millions of people clad in white attire in this place worshiping God with a vigor that I have never witnessed upon the earth. The experience of being in the throne room changed my life. Yes, heaven is real!

CHAPTER 30

The Lord's Righteous Judgments and Eternal Grace

Once I turned to see Jesus smiling at me as I was looking around examining my surroundings. My investigation seemed to cause a bright smile to fill the Lord's face. The Lord placed His hand upon my back again. This supernaturally strengthened me and gave me courage to move even closer to the throne. After some time we began to draw closer to the throne. The sound of the worship was so loud and intense that the very ground under my feet seemed to quake. It was then that I began to notice angelic beings that were flying around the throne. The colors and the glory that emanated from the throne made it difficult to look at the throne for no longer than a second or two.

However, it appeared to me that these angels were moving acrobatically in and through the glory surrounding the throne. They were singing and worshipping loudly and with a supernatural passion. As these angels darted about, their multifaceted wings dispersed the glory of God in all directions at once. Phosphorescent colors cascaded in all directions around the throne to be reflected by the crystal cathedral and the waters surrounding the throne. Perhaps these were seraphim or cherubim. I am in no way certain, but these angelic beings worshiped the Lord and their wings cascaded God's glory in every direction as they flew acrobatically around the throne.

As we drew nearer I saw that the Father's throne was surrounded by other much smaller very luxuriant chairs which seemed to be constructed of gold and red velvet. Of this I am not sure. Each chair was of Victorian looking design and had very ornate carvings upon the arms and legs. These chairs were quite large by earth's standards and had similar styled footstools at each one. It dawned upon me that these may have been the twenty-four elders spoken of in Revelation. Again, I am not certain and this is total speculation on my part. Although, when I sought to look at them I was unable to see them clearly as they were bathed in brilliant light and glory. Jesus continued to walk up to the throne. When we reached the bottom of the platform I saw twelve large stairs leading up to the throne area. These large stairs seemed to be made of gemstones like diamonds, rubies, sapphires, mother of pearl, topaz, emerald, turquoise, amethyst, and others perhaps, but I am not sure. They emanated the glory and lights around the throne with brilliant reflections. Each step was about eighteen inches in height.

For a moment I discerned the words "mercy and justice" flashed upon these foundational steps of the throne. When Jesus began to walk up the steps I noticed that there was a magnificent place established for Him on the right hand of the Father. Remaining at the bottom of the throne I stood still like a statue paralyzed by the reverential fear of God and the intense glory. Thunder once more roared in my ears and lightening bolted over my head at that instant illuminating the ceiling and the crystalline waters as Jesus sat down upon His throne. I closed my eyes and fell upon my face and remained in that position for a long time. I entered into the worship of the Lord with all of my spirit and soul, and the sensation was exhilarating and amazing as we sang. *"Worthy is the Lamb who was slain to receive power and riches and wisdom, And strength and honor and glory and blessing!"* (Revelation 5:12).

After a long time a persistent buzzing sound filled my ears, and I looked up to see a large angelic being hovering near my head. It was similar to the angels that I had seen at the place I call the vault of mantles. Slowly I rose up upon my knees to see the cherubim dart back into the phosphorescent glory of the Father that was radiating around the throne. In this place the tangible fear of the Lord was overwhelming, and for a moment I wondered if I was going to live. I wondered why the Lord had brought me to this magnificent place. Would I live, or would this be the day that I stood before the throne of God's judgment and grace?

Melchizedek

At that instant I looked up to see Jesus sitting upon His throne in His rightful place at the right hand of the Father. The Lord smiled at me, and once again hope bubbled up within my spirit that I might live and not die. Jesus motioned for me to join Him. Astonished, I stood up on my wobbly legs and walked slowly up the twelve stairs to stand beside the right hand side of Jesus (Revelation 3:21). My senses were overloaded by the sights and sounds surrounding the throne. The power of God's glory in this place is impossible for me to describe accurately. The volume of the sounds and the sheer size of this crystal cathedral of God were too much for my human mind to comprehend in that moment.

It took a long time, but gradually I began to adjust to the overwhelming and tangible presence of the glory that was radiating from this place. Jesus made a gesture to me with His chin indicating that I should turn around and look out into this massive room. Today I believe that I was totally invisible as I stood there and no one else in the room saw me. I had been watching and observing Jesus for a long time. I was totally absorbed in the majesty and grandeur of the Messiah as He sat upon the throne. Truly Jesus *is the* High Priest forever according to the order of Melchizedek (Psalm 110:4; Hebrews 6:20). I did not want to leave His presence nor did I wish to look at anything else in this place save for my Savior. There was no need to pray or even think. I just wanted to luxuriate in being here in the very presence of the Most High God and worshipping the Lord with my entire being.

At that moment I realized that tears were flowing from my eyes and my heart was burning with a love and passion for God that I had never known. I looked into the eyes of Jesus again. Once more the Lord smiled at me, and He raised His chin slightly for a second time indicating that I should look around. I turned around to look upon the masses of people that were gathered around the throne. Below the river of God reflected the glory of the throne in unison and in harmony with the vaulted crystal ceilings of this amazing and magnificent room. These created perfect acoustics for the worship that was ongoing in this massive crystal cathedral. Millions and millions of saints in white robes were arranged in a massive circle around the Father's throne. God's angels of various kinds were worshipping the Lord in unison with these saints. There were balconies at various levels where angels sang and played musical instruments worshipping God in spirit and in truth in unison with the millions of saints below.

The throne room was perhaps miles in circumference. At one point I heard a massive clap of thunder and I realized that something was about to transpire. Perhaps this was what the Lord had wanted for me to witness. My attention was drawn to the area in front of the center of the platform which surrounds the throne. I saw a young man approach the throne of the Lord and he was accompanied by several angels. His head was bowed and he was trembling in great fear. Somehow I knew that it was time for this man to stand before God. I saw two large books brought to the Father's throne by angelic beings. I understood that these books were this person's books of life. The books in the angel's hands were similar to the millions of books that I had seen in the place I called the Father's library earlier.

CHAPTER 31

The Author and Finisher of Faith

One of the elders came forward and began to read from one of the books. This man's stature was very regal and his hair was so white that it seemed to glow. His words were clear and pronounced and articulated perfectly. The elder spoke for what seemed like hours sharing in great detail events from the man's life. As he spoke images of the events depicted were visible above the throne. All the while the glory of God emanated and shot out from around the throne. I heard a sound and saw Jesus rise up and walk down to stand beside the man at the foot of the throne. The Lord began to speak on the young man's behalf. I was not able to understand the words that Jesus was saying but I understood that Jesus was making a defense for this man. Jesus acted as his advocate just as a trial lawyer would defend someone in a court of law upon the earth.

This man had made Christ his Savior on earth and had not denied the Lord. And at this moment Jesus was defending him before the Father as Abba Father sat upon His throne. This man's sins had been washed clean by the blood of the Messiah. He was about to enter into heaven for eternity as Christ spoke upon his behalf. Perhaps what I was seeing was what Jesus referred to as the resurrection of the just in Luke, chapter 14. In that passage the Lord referred to how people of the earth would receive a reward in heaven for their genuine benevolent acts upon earth.

As I watched this scene unfold before me I understood that this man's gifts to the poor and alms were coming up before the Father (Acts 10:4). I also understood that he was going to reap a heavenly reward for the things that he had done during his earthly life to help those who were less fortunate than him. I watched as this man received a beautiful crown of righteousness from one of the elders in attendance. At the command of Christ, two angels came forward to place a brilliant white robe upon the young man's shoulders. The young man then turned to join the millions who began to worship God in unison. I was amazed by what I was experiencing.

Jesus as Savior and Messiah

After a moment the Lord returned to His place at the right hand of the Father. However, over the next several hours I watched this scenario play itself out time and time again. I may have actually been in this place for days, but later when I returned to my prayer room I was surprised to find that only about nine hours had passed. I must have witnessed hundreds of individuals come to stand before the throne of the Father.

I watched as their lives were played out in the midst of the heavenly realms. For each one of those who knew Jesus as Savior and Messiah, I saw Jesus stand and speak upon their behalf. The Lord stated their case that they might be acquitted and their iniquities imputed before the Father. Jesus would defend them and the many were granted new robes and some received crowns of righteousness (James 1:2; 2 Timothy 2:4; 1 Peter

5:4; Revelation 2:10). I understood that their sins were no longer recorded in their book of life, and they were given heavenly rewards and crowns of righteousness. I saw many saints who received these beautiful golden and jeweled crowns of life and righteousness lay these heavenly treasures at the feet of Jesus before the Father's throne (Revelation 4:10).

Each time this transpired the entire congregation of millions would begin to praise Jesus saying (Revelation 5:12-13),

> *Worthy is the Lamb who was slain To receive power and riches and wisdom, And strength and honor and glory and blessing!...Blessing and honor and glory and power Be to Him who sits on the throne, and to the Lamb, forever and ever!*

Then there would be a thunderous chorus of "amen," and the whole family of God would worship the Lord once more. I witnessed this dynamic transpire time and time again.

After I had witnessed several people approach the throne to stand before the one true holy and righteous God, it occurred to me that these individuals' eternal destinies were being decided. The Lord was rewarding them based upon the choices that each had made and how they had lived their earthly lives. An intense desire to pray for each one welled up inside of me, and I began to intercede for each one in turn. Some did not receive new robes or crowns of righteousness. It appeared that Jesus wept when this happened, and I would pray all the more. After a long time I turned to see Jesus motion to me calling me to Himself.

His Burning Eyes of Eternal Love

I walked over to look into the eyes of the Lord. As I gazed into His burning eyes of eternal love, understanding filled my heart of the magnitude of the sacrifice He had made for all of mankind. I began to weep and morn for those who were turned away. I saw that many were cast into what appeared to be outer darkness (Matthew 8:12; 25:30). I held my face in my hands as if to hide my tears from the Lord, and then I felt the Lord place His gentle warm hands upon my shoulders. I looked up to see Jesus looking deeply and passionately into my eyes. He said, "Consider carefully what you have seen and heard here today. Write down all things that you have seen and heard, and remember you are always welcome here."

I understood that every tongue, tribe, and nation is welcome to be in this place with God too. In fact, of this I am certain: all people will one day stand in this place. You will stand before God's throne and give an account too (Romans 14:10-12; 1 Peter 4:5; Acts 10:42; 2 Timothy 4:1; 2 Corinthians 5:10).

Think about that.

CHAPTER 32

God's Unconditional, Unimaginable, and Indescribable Love

The Lord smiled and embraced me once more. As He wrapped His arms of love around me, I was filled with the sense of God's unconditional, unimaginable, and indescribable love for me once again. The sensation was similar the night of November 25, 2001, when the Lord Jesus stood over me in Newfoundland and I had been filled with understanding of the Messiah's unbelievable love for all of mankind.

Jesus released me from His tender embrace and smiled at me one last time. Then Jesus descended down the twelve steps once more to meet a new arrival at the foot of the Father's throne of mercy, judgment, and grace. I fell to my knees and began to pray for the young woman who stood at the foot of God's throne alone. She reminded me of my daughters. She appeared to quake with fear and trembling. When I rose up I was back in my prayer room, and tears were pooling on the old shag carpet below me. The fragrances of frankincense and myrrh lingered in the air and I could still hear that angelic worship swirling around me. I remained upon my knees weeping and interceding for various people for a long time. Later, I began to ponder these things in my heart and searched my old

King James Bible for answers. Nearly twenty years have passed since this event occurred. I felt that it was very important that I share this testimony with you, the reader, in the conclusion of this book.

At times the Kingdom of God is often a conundrum. In Christ's Kingdom it can be both and concerning many issues. I have often thought of Ephesians, chapter 2, when I have pondered this visit to the throne room in my heart over the years. Verses 5 through 9 in that passage say:

> Even when we were dead in trespasses,[God] made us alive together with Christ (by grace you have been saved), and raised us up together, and made us sit together in the heavenly places in Christ Jesus, that in the ages to come He might show the exceeding riches of His grace in His kindness toward us in Christ Jesus. For by grace you have been saved through faith, and that not of yourselves; it is the gift of God, not of works, lest anyone should boast.

No Other Name

Surely the salvation that God had given mankind comes from the finished work of the Messiah and Savior, Jesus Christ of Nazareth. And there is no other name by which men might be saved and restored to right relationship to God. Salvation is a gift of grace, no doubt. However, the Scriptures also tell us that everyone who will ever live upon the earth will stand before the throne of God. King Solomon stated this matter well in Ecclesiastes 12:13-14 saying:

God's Unconditional, Unimaginable, and Indescribable Love

> *Let us hear the conclusion of the whole matter: Fear God and keep His commandment, For this is man's all. For God will bring every work into judgment, Including every secret thing, Whether good or evil.*

Jesus Himself spoke of the judgment day in Matthew 12:36-37, teaching us:

> *But I say to you that for every idle word men may speak, they will give account of it in the day of judgment. For by your words you will be justified, and by your words you will be condemned.*

In fact, Scripture is replete with examples of how we will all stand before God one day. (Also see Ecclesiastes 12:14; Luke 9:26; 14:14; Acts 10:42; 17:31; Romans 2:6, 16; 14:10-12; 1 Corinthians 3:8; 2 Corinthians 5:10-11; Matthew 7:21-23; 16:27; 25:31; 26:64; Mark 8:38; John 5:22; 12:48; 2 Timothy 4:1; 1 Peter 4:5; Revelation 2:23; 20:12; 22:12).

Perhaps in His mercy and grace the Lord allowed me to witness the throne and a tiny portion of the resurrection of the just. Perhaps Revelation 20:11-12 depicts the best confirmation to the throne room encounter that I experienced:

> *Then I saw a great white throne and Him who sat on it, from whose face the earth and the heaven fled away. And there was found no place for them. And I saw the dead, small and great, standing before God, and books were opened. And another book was opened, which is the Book of Life. And the dead were judged according to their works, by the things which were written in the books.*

I am certain of one thing. Heaven is real and God wants you to spend eternity there. I remained in prayer for another full day considering everything I had seen and heard just as Jesus had instructed me. I searched the Scriptures seeking confirmation. I have often asked myself this question: what will happen on the day that I stand before my heavenly Father? I have considered this question for many years, and I continue to ponder these things in my heart even today.

What about you? Have you considered these things? Are you 100 percent sure about where you will stand with God when you find yourself before the throne of the Father? Will Jesus stand at your side as your Advocate and mighty Counselor (Isaiah 9:6; 1 John 2:1)? If you are not certain where you stand before God perhaps you may wish to pray the prayer at the end of this chapter, because heaven is real.

As of this writing nearly seventeen years have passed. There is one thing that I know to be true. Jesus Christ is not dead.

No.

Jesus Christ of Nazareth is alive and He loves you with an everlasting love that you cannot imagine. In fact, Jesus loves every tribe every tongue and every nation upon the earth. He is a friend who will stick closer to you than a brother and He has laid down His life for you.

Jesus died that you might live.

Jesus' teaching in John 15:13 speaks of real love: *"Greater love has no one than this, than to lay down one's life for his friends."*

In 1 John 3:16, John the Revelator gives us insight into the love of the Lord Jesus for you: *"By this we know love, because*

He laid down His life for us. And we also ought to lay down our lives for the brethren."

Yes.

Jesus gave up His life that we might live on for eternity in heaven.

Heaven is real.

Prayer Index

Prayer of Salvation

The Word of God gives us simple steps to become a new creation and to enter into God's family.

You can inherit eternal life and live forever more in paradise or heaven.

If you believe in your heart that Jesus Christ of Nazareth was the Son of the living God and that He died upon the Cross to pay for your sins, you can be saved.

Romans 10:10 tells you how to be "born again": *"With the heart one believes unto righteousness, and with the mouth confession is made unto salvation."*

If you believe this just pray this simple prayer:

Dear heavenly Father, I confess Jesus Christ as Lord. I believe with all of my heart that Jesus is the Son of God and that He shed His blood and was crucified to pay for my sins. I believe that Jesus did rise from the dead on the third day. I believe that Jesus is alive, and that He will save me now. Lord, I am a sinner. I ask you to forgive my sins and to save me right now. In Jesus' name I pray, amen.

Lord, I thank You that I am saved! I am a new creature, and I am now in the family of God. I have become the righteousness of God!

If you prayed that prayer, we want to hear from you and to send you a free gift from King of Glory Ministries International. Send us your address and we will gladly send a free gift to congratulate you on your decision!

Prayer of Impartation of the Seer Operation

Put your hand on your chest and pray out loud:

Lord, I ask You to reveal to me the secrets and hidden mysteries that eye has not seen and ear has not heard. Lord, I ask in Jesus' name that You ignite my heart by the power of Your Spirit. Lord, let the Kingdom of Heaven enter into my heart. Father, I'm asking You to reveal to me the mysteries and the secret things that You have prepared for those who love You. And, Lord, I love You. I ask You, Father, in the name of Jesus, to reveal the fellowship of the mysteries of the unsearchable riches found in Jesus Christ. Lord, I ask that You reveal them to me. Reveal them to my spirit. Lord, I ask that You open up to me the manifold wisdom of God. Lord, I'm asking that You would give me eyes to see and ears to hear. Lord, I'm asking that You would release to me spiritual discernment to see and to hear in a new and supernatural way. Holy Spirit, I welcome You to try me. Father God, I ask You to create within me a clean heart and renew a steadfast spirit within me. In Jesus' name I pray, amen.

Prayer of Activation

Father, I thank You for the wonderful saints reading this now. I pray right now, Lord, and I ask that You would fill us with the knowledge of Your will for each of us. Lord, I ask that You would release to us wisdom and spiritual understanding. Father, I'm asking that You would help us to discern, to see, to taste, to smell, to touch the unseen realm. I ask, Father God, in Jesus' name, that You would give us spiritual understanding. I cover each of us in the blood of Jesus. I ask You, Father God, that we would see nothing except what You would have us to see; that we would have no visions, no dreams, no trances, no supernatural encounters except those that were ordained by God the Father, God the Son, and God the Holy Spirit. And, Lord, I thank You that the heavens are open in this place, right now.

Lord, Your angels are welcome to descend even now to minister for those who are heirs of salvation. Father, we thank You that it is fully pleasing to You that each of us would be fruitful in every good work and that we would increase in the knowledge of You.

Father, I ask You today that we would be strengthened with Your might and Your glorious power. Father, I thank You that we are already qualified through the blood of Jesus Christ and the finished work of the Cross to be partakers of our heavenly inheritance as saints of light.

Lord, I ask that You would convey us even now into the invisible realms of the Kingdom of Your Son, the Lord Jesus Christ of Nazareth. Help me to discern and entertain heaven right now, Lord.

Father, I just thank You that we have an inheritance of light that we can access through the finished work of Jesus Christ on the Cross. Father, we thank You that the Cross of Jesus is the bridge that opens up the heavenly places to us. And, Lord, I thank You that we are seated in the heavenly places with Christ Jesus. Lord, we give You the praise and the honor and the glory for everything You've done, everything You are doing, and everything You are going to do, in Jesus' mighty name, amen.

Notes

Chapter 3 ~ Heaven Is Real

1. "I'm Just an Old Chunk of coal (But I'm Going to be a Diamond Someday" is a song written by Billy Joe Shaver in 1981 as a "metaphor to represent his faith in Jesus." He recorded it, as did John Anderson, Johnny Cash, and Kris Kristofferson: http://www.songfacts.com/detail.php?id=20755.

Chapter 4 ~ Heavenly Dimensions

1. Helen Barrett Montgomery, *The Centenary Translation of the New Testament* (Philadelphia: The American Baptist Publication Society, 1924).

Chapter 10 ~ The Hidden and Mysterious Treasures of the Kingdom of Heaven

1. "Earth's day length shortened by Japan earthquake," *CBS News.com*, March 13, 2011, https://www.cbsnews.com/news/earths-day-length-shortened-by-japan-earthquake/; Staff, "How the Japan Earthquake Shortened Days on Earth," *Space.com*, March 13, 2011, https://www.space.com/11115-japan-earthquake-shortened-earth-days.html; Doyle Rice, "NASA: Japan quake shortened Earth's day, shifted axis," *USA Today*, March 13, 2011, http://content.usatoday.com/communities/sciencefair/post/2011/03/

japan-earthquake-shifted-earth-axis-shorter-day-nasa/1#. WaB9izuQyUk (accessed October 25, 2017).

Chapter 14 ~ Entertaining Heaven

1. "How Many People Have ever Lived on Earth?" *Population Reference Bureau*, http://www.prb.org/Publications/Articles/2002/HowManyPeopleHaveEverLivedonEarth.aspx (accessed October 25, 2017).
2. "Current World Population," *Worldometers*, http://www.worldometers.info/world-population/ (accessed October 25, 2017).

Contact the Authors

Kevin and Kathy would love to hear your testimonies for possible use in future publications.

To submit testimonies contact them at their email address below:

Email: info@kingofgloryministries.org.
Phone: 336-818-1210 or 828-320-3502

Mailing Address:
King of Glory Ministries International
P O Box 903, Moravian Falls, NC 28654

King of Glory Ministries International
has the material on this book available for study groups.

These schools are available in DVD and CD sets and online at our School of Higher Learning. Visit the Moravian Falls School of Higher Learning at www.moravianfallsschoolofhigherlearning.org

For more information or to order additional resources of books
Please visit our Web page at:
www.kingofgloryministries.org

About the Authors and King of Glory Ministries International

Kevin and Kathy Basconi are ordinary people who love an extraordinary God. They co-founded King of Glory Ministries International. They have a heart to share the Gospel with the poor and the love of the Father to widows and orphans. They have visited thirty-three nations preaching the Gospel and demonstrating the Kingdom of God in churches, conferences, and crusade meetings. The ministry is punctuated by many miracles, healings, and signs and wonders that confirm the Word of God. They live in the mountains where they pursue a lifestyle of intimacy with Jesus.

Kevin is an internationally published author and award winning artist. He is the author of several books including the trilogy *Unlocking the Hidden Mysteries of the Seer Anointing books 1, 2, & 3* and *The Sword of the Lord*. Kevin's bestselling books, *Visitations of Angels and Other Supernatural Experiences Volume #1 & #2* are available through King of Glory Ministries International. Kevin has been graced by God to see into the spiritual realm for over a decade and often sees and discerns angelic activity. Kevin is called to equip the Body of Christ to operate in the "seer anointing" and to help people understand how to enter into the presence and glory of God. You can learn more information about Kevin and Kathy at **www.kingofgloryministries.org**

Kevin is an ordained minister accredited with World Ministry Fellowship of Plano, Texas.

King of Glory Ministries International is also connected to the apostolic leadership of Pastors Alan and Carol Koch of Christ Triumphant Church located In Lee's Summit, Missouri.

King of Glory Ministries International is all about the commission of Jesus Christ. The words of Isaiah 61, verses 1-3, can be used to concisely summarize the call of the ministry:

> *The Spirit of the Lord GOD is upon Me, Because the LORD has anointed Me To preach good tidings to the poor; He has sent Me to heal the brokenhearted, To proclaim liberty to the captives, And the opening of the prison to those who are bound; To proclaim the acceptable year of the LORD, And the day of vengeance of our God; To comfort all who mourn, To console those who mourn in Zion, To give them beauty for ashes, The oil of joy for mourning, The garment of praise for the spirit of heaviness; That they may be called trees of righteousness, The planting of the LORD, that He may be glorified.*

We have sought to preach the Gospel of the Kingdom to the lost in many nations. As of this writing we have visited over thirty nations and five continents to proclaim the truth of Christ's total salvation and healing message, or the Gospel of the Kingdom that Jesus instructed His disciples to proclaim. (See Matthew 4:23; 9:35; 24:14.) We have preached to hundreds of thousands of people and seen tens of thousands make the decision to receive Jesus Christ as Lord and Savior. We continue to minister in large crusade outreaches in Africa and other nations today as opportunity allows and as the Spirit leads. Kevin and Kathy also minister in churches, King of Glory Ministries International Schools, and conference meetings in various nations.

The other critical calling of King of Glory Ministries International is to minister the love of the Father to widows and orphans. This humanitarian aspect of our call can be defined in the scriptures of James 1:27 and Psalm 68:5. James 1:27 tells us this:

> *Pure and undefiled religion before God and the Father is this: to visit orphans and widows in their trouble, and to keep oneself unspotted from the world.*

God has birthed in Kevin and Kathy a heart to minister in deed and not word alone. We also see this aspect of the Father's heart in Psalm 68:5:

> *A father of the fatherless, a defender of widows, Is God in His holy habitation.*

For more information on King of Glory Ministries and their orphan outreaches, visit their Web page at www.kingofglory-ministries.org.

Other Books by Kevin Basconi

**Visitations of Angels
& Other Supernatural Encounters Volume #1**

**Visitations of Angels
& Other Supernatural Encounters Volume #2**

31 Word Decrees That Can Revolutionize Your Life

**Unlocking the Hidden Mysteries
of the Seer Anointing–Book I**

**Unlocking the Hidden Mysteries of the Seer Anointing 2
and the Blessings of Psalm 24–Book II**

**Unlocking the Hidden Mysteries of the Seer Anointing and
the Powers of the Age to Come –Book III**

The Sword of the Lord & The Rest of the Lord

Coming soon:
365 Word Decrees that Can Revolutionize Your Life

To order ALL of these titles in PDF Format or on Kindle or iTunes, please visit our online resource store.
Also visit our store for dozens of audio teachings at

www.kingofgloryministries.org/store

Order by phone:
336-818-1210

Visit our new online **free** mentoring school featuring over 300 hours of audio, video, and written teachings.

The Moravian Falls School of Higher Learning

Preaching the Gospel of the Kingdom to the ends of the earth from the very heart of Moravian Falls, North Carolina

www.moravianfallsschoolofhigherlearning.org

Always on, always **free**

Please visit our online book store for more resources from King of Glory Ministries International

At this link:

https://kingofgloryministries.org/store

Visitation 2 for 1 Bundle
Limited Offer!

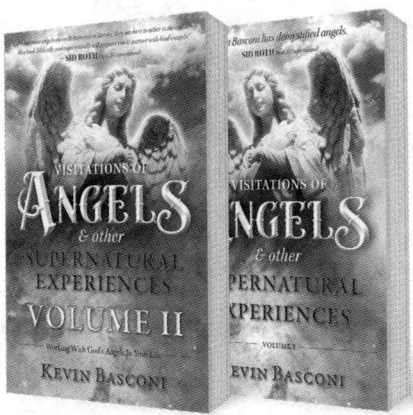

Great offer on Kevin's best selling books! Get two for the price of one for a limited time!

Searching for angels? Prepare to find them in the pages of these books. Travel with me around the world from Israel to South America, Africa, and South Korea and beyond as I share testimonies of modern day angelic encounters that I have experienced over last fifteen years. This amazing book will help you learn and understand how to: Activate Gods angels of protection in your life and sphere of influence Co-labor with God's angels of supernatural provision in the glory realms and much more!

$40.00

SALE $18.99

Seer Trilogy Book Bundle
Limited Offer!

Learn how to see into the unseen realm and discern God's Angels! Get the entire Seer Trilogy for one great price! Now for a limited time only Get all three of these powerful books on the Seer Operation for this great price.

~~$60.00~~

SALE $27.99

From the Gutter to Glory
New Release

In this powerful little book Kevin Basconi shares his testimony or redemption and deliverance. This is a real look at what salvation can really mean in the life of one who has a contrite and broken spirit.

This little book was nearly twenty years in the making. In it Kevin Basconi takes the reader on a supernatural journey into the Kingdom of God. The Scripture teaches us this unchangeable fact: "the testimony of Jesus is the spirit of prophesy". In this fast-paced testimonial book, Kevin shares how his life was transformed by supernatural encounters and heavenly experiences.

~~$7.99~~

SALE $3.99

This book was prepared for printing by

King of Glory Printing & Publishing

Our goal is to help unpublished authors facilitate printing of their manuscripts in a professional and economical way. If you have a manuscript you would like to have printed, contact us:

336-818-1210
or
828-320-3502

PO BOX 903
Moravian Falls, NC 28654

www.kingofgloryministries.org